AYURVEDA QUESTION BANK

For AYUSH NET Ph.D.

Amrit Pal Singh Saroya

SCIENTIFIC PUBLISHERS

Published by:

SCIENTIFIC PUBLISHERS (INDIA)
5A, New Pali Road, P.O. Box 91
Jodhpur 342 001, India
E-mail: info@scientificpub.com
Website: www.scientificpubonline.com

Print 2026

ISBN: 978-93-90749-68-3
eISBN: 978-93-90749-69-0

Printed in India

PREFACE

Ph.D. or doctorate degree in Ayurveda is an old tradition. Several universities and national institutes are offering full time or part time Ph.D. or doctorate degree in AYUSH systems of medicine. Until the introduction of AYUSH Ph.D. Fellowship scheme, no standardized guidelines either framed by AYUSH or CCIM were nonexistent. Introduction of AYUSH Ph.D. Fellowship/ Senior Research Scheme is a welcome move in enhancing the credibility of AYUSH systems of medicine. It provides a suitable platform for advance studies after post graduation i.e. M.D. degree.

Based on topics prescribed for Ayurveda portion, an attempt has been made to create question bank based on multiple choice questions (MCQs) for aspiring students appearing in the entrance examination for AYUSH Ph.D. Fellowship scheme. No formal syllabus has been designed for the entrance test held every year. However, based on the topics prescribed on priority areas of research, several books, journals and databases of national and international importance have been screened for extraction of relevant data. 500 questions have been selected related to priority areas of research have been included in the question bank and shall be expanded in near future based on the market feedback.

Several universities are conducting Pre Ph.D. entrance test for candidates not eligible for AYUSH Ph.D. Fellowship scheme due to age bar. Recently, Guru Ravi Dass Ayurvedic University, Hoshiarpur and Shri Krishna AYUSH University, Kurukshetra have conducted debut entrance test leading to admission in Ph.D. The question bank shall be of great utility for aspirants seeking admission in Ph.D.

Phytochemistry offered by Uttrakhand Ayurvedic University, Dehradun. Research methodology has been excluded from the question bank keeping in mind the scope.

I sincerely hope that the work titled 'Question Bank AYUSH NET Ph.D. Fellowship/Senior Research shall be of great service for students seeking admission in various disciplines of Ayurveda.

Authors

AYUSH Ph.D. FELLOWHSIP SCHEME

On 26th October, 2016 University Grants Commission (UGC) issued advisory vide D.O. No. F. 14-12/2016 (CPP-II) to the vice chancellors of Indian universities for inclusion of AYUSH disciplines in the universities and affiliated colleges for enrolment of candidates in the Ph.D studies and availing the fellowship from the concerned apex body i.e. AYUSH research council (CCRAS, CCH, CCRUM, and CCRS).

University Grants Commission has credited mutual recognition to UGC-NET and AYUSH-NET VIDE D.O. No. F. 21-2/2016 (PS/PMO/PG) for admission to Ph.D. programs in AYUSH except for those subjects in which UGC is conducting net. Accordingly, the Department of AYUSH requested the Vice Chancelors of the universities and Directors of the Institutes for extending exemption to AYUSH-NET qualified candidates from the entrance test conducted by the university and affiliated colleges on lines similar to UGC-NET AND CSIR-NET.

AYUSH Ph.D. FELLOWHSIP SCHEME-AYURVEDA

Central Council for Research in Ayurvedic Sciences (CCRAS) under ministry of AYUSH provide research fellowship to bright professionals in methods of research under the guidance of faculty/scientist working in Department of Government Universities/ Institutes of National Importance/National Laboratories/Institutes of Research Councils in various fields of Science and Technology and Medical Sciences, particularly AYUSH systems.

THE PRIORTIES AREA OF RESEARCH

- Clinical Research

- Fundamental Research
- Literary Research
- Ayurvedic Pharmaceutics
- Extrapharmacopoeial Drugs
- Ayurveda relation to other subjects.

Multiple Choice Questions

- Ayurveda relation to other subjects
- Ayurvedic pharmaceutical Sciences
- Clinical trials
- Drug & Cosmetic Act
- Extrapharmacopoeial drugs
- Heavy metal issues
- Metallic preparations
- Preclinical research
- Regulatory Affairs
- Standardization
- Toxicity studies

1. The comprehensive study of crude vegetable drugs is known as:

(A) Materia Medica

(B) Homeopathic Materia Medica

(C) Ethnopharmacology

(D) Phytochemistry

2. Which of the following academic subjects of modern medicine equates well with *Dravyaguna*?

(A) Pharmacognosy and pharmacology

(B) Pharmacognosy and phytochemistry

(C) Pharmacology

(D) Clinical pharmacology

3. The study of chemical composition of the herbal drugs is addressed as

(A) Phytochemistry (B) Latrochemistry

(C) Organic chemistry (D) Natural Product Chemistry

4. As per Central Council of India (C.C.I.M) guidelines, subject (s) allied to *Dravyaguna* are:

(A) Agadtantra

(B) Rasa Shastra avam Bhaishajya Kalpana

(C) Both of the above

(D) None of the above

5. As per Central Council of India (C.C.I.M) M.S.R., total built area of Herbarium-cum Dravyaguna Museum and Pharmacognosy and Pharmacology laboratory for 100 students capacity should be

(A) 250 sq.m. (B) 500 sq.m.

(C) 650 sq.m. (D) 800 sq.m.

6. Postgraduate Diploma in Dravyaguna initiated by Central Council of India (C.C.I.M) is regulated by which regulations?

(A) Indian Medicine Central Council (Permission to existing Colleges) Regulations, 2006,

(B) Indian Medicine Central Council (Post-graduate Diploma Course) (Ayurveda) Regulations 2010,

(C) Indian Medicine Central Council (Minimum Standard Requirements of Ayurveda Colleges and attached Hospitals) Regulations, 2016,

(D) Indian Medicine Central Council (Minimum standards of Education in Indian Medicine) Amendment Regulations, 2019.

7. M.Pharm qualification in *Dravyaguna* is offered by which of the following universities?

(A) Lovely Professional University, Phagwara

(B) Shri Krishna AYUSH University, Kurukshetra

(C) Guru Ravi Das Ayurvedic University, Hoshiarpur

(D) Uttrakhand Ayurvedic University, Dehradun.

8. M.Pharm qualification in *Dravyaguna* is recognized by

(A) Central Council of Indian Medicine

(B) Pharmacy Council of India

(C) Department of AYUSH

(D) Unrecognized qualification.

9. M.D. *Dravyaguna* degree course is regulated by which of the following Acts of Central Council of Indian Medicine afresh?

(A) The Indian Medicine Central Council (Post Graduate Education Ayurveda) Regulations, 1994,

(B) The Indian Medicine Central Council (Post Graduate Education Ayurveda) Regulations, 2012,

(C) The Indian Medicine Central Council (Post Graduate Education Ayurveda) Regulations, 2016,

(D) The Indian Medicine Central Council (Post Graduate Education Ayurveda) Amendment Regulations, 2019.

10. M.S. (Pharm) Course in Traditional Medicine was initiated in 2007 by which of the following institutes?

(A) National Institute of Pharmaceutical Education and Research, Mohali

(B) Gujarat Ayurved University, Jamnagar

(C) Rajasthan Ayurved University, Jodhpur

(D) Uttrakhand Ayurvedic University, Dehradun

11. The herbal garden attached to the Dravayguna department of the Ayurvedic College admitting 100 students should have how many medicinal species?

(A) 150 (B) 200

(C) 250 (D) 300

12. Which of the following apex body deals with research policy on Ayurvedic drugs?

(A) Central Council for Research in Ayurvedic Sciences (CCRAS)

(B) Central Council of Indian Medicine (CCIM)

(C) Department of AYUSH

(D) AYUSH Task Force

13. Extramural Research Projects in AYUSH systems of medicine are funded by which of the following?

(A) Department of AYUSH

(B) Central Council for Research in Ayurvedic Sciences (CCRAS)

(C) Centre for Research in Indian Systems of Medicine (CRISM)

(D) All of the above

14. The publication named 'AYURVEDIC DOSSIER' has been published by which of the following?

(A) Central Council for Research in Ayurvedic Sciences (CCRAS)

(B) Department of AYUSH

(C) Central Council of Indian Medicine (CCIM)

(D) None of the above

15. Which of the following body advises the government on issues related to the ASU drugs?

(A) Ayurveda, Siddha, Unani Drugs Technical Advisory Board (ASUDTAB)

(B) Ayurveda, Siddha, Unani Drugs Consultative Committee (ASUDCC)

(C) State licensing authorities

(D) All of the above

16. Which of the following body advises the government on issues related to implementation?

(A) Ayurveda, Siddha, Unani Drugs Technical Advisory Board (ASUDTAB)

(B) Ayurveda, Siddha, Unani Drugs Consultative Committee (ASUDCC)

(C) State licensing authorities

(D) None of the above

17. Essential Drug List (EDL) for Ayurvedic drugs and formulations was launched in which year?

(A) 2012 (B) 2013

(C) 2015 (D) 2019

18. Ayurvedic Pharmacopoeia of India (API) describes assay, purity and potency of which of the following?

(A) Single herb (B) Polyherbal

(C) Minerals (D) Metals

19. The analytical description of formulations used in Ayurveda is mentioned in which of the following texts?

(A) Ayurvedic Formulary of India

(B) Ayurvedic Pharmacopoeia of India

(C) Essential Drug List

(D) Pharmacopoeial standards of Indian Drugs.

20. The Department of AYUSH was formerly known as:

(A) Department of Indian System of Medicine (ISM)

(B) Department of Indian System of Medicine & Homeopathy (ISM&H)

(C) Department of Ayurved, Siddha & Unani (ASU)

(D) None of the above.

21. Which system of medicine has been given official recognition by Central Council of Indian Medicine recently?

(A) Amachi (B) Unani

(C) Siddha (D) Homeopathy

22. Specimen dipped in 15 gm of mercuric chloride mixed with which of the following for preventing spoilage and decomposition?

(A) 70% alcohol (B) Ethyl alcohol

(C) Absolute alcohol (D) Isopropyl alcohol

23. Solution containing------------------part of formaldehyde and -----------------parts of 70% alcohol is used for poisoning the plant material:

(A) 1 and 2 (B) 1 and 3

(C) 3 and 4 (D) 2 and 3.

24. Which of the following is ideal repellent for herbarium sheets?

(A) 2 parts of naphthalene compound and one part of paradichloro benzene

(B) Naphthalene compound alone

(C) Paradichloro benzene alone

(D) All of the above.

25. Which of the following are used as insecticides for herbarium sheets?

(A) Carbon disulphide (B) Cyanide gas

(C) Ethylene dichloride (D) All of the above.

26. Ministry of AYUSH in collaboration with Food Safety and Standards Authority of India (FSSAI) is bringing a new regulation on food named Ayurveda under the name:

(A) Aahar (B) AYUSH aahar

(C) Ayurvedic foods (D) AYUSH foods.

27. Which of the following publications have been carried out by Central Council for Research in Ayurvedic Sciences (CCRAS)?

(A) General Guidelines for Safety/Toxicity Evaluation of Ayurvedic Formulations

(B) General Guidelines for Clinical Evaluation of Evaluation Interventions

(C) General Guidelines for Drug Development of Ayurvedic Formulations

(D) All of the above.

28. The first edition of document "CCRAS Research Policy" was published in which of the following years?

(A) 2012 (B) 2015

(C) 2017 (D) 2018.

29. CCRAS Policy for Commercialization of Technologies was formulated in which of the following years?

(A) 2012 (B) 2014

(C) 2017 (D) 2018.

30. The first edition of document "Pre Accreditation Entry Level Standards for AYUSH Hospitals" has been formulated by which of the following institutes?

(A) National Accreditation Board for Hospitals and Healthcare Providers (NABH)

(B) Department of AYUSH

(C) Central Council for Research in Ayurvedic Sciences (CCRAS)

(D) Ministry of Health and Family Welfare

31. Interdisciplinary AYUSH Research and Development Taskforce set up for the purpose of screening of projects related to COVID 19 is functional under the umbrella of

(A) Department of AYUSH

(B) Central Council for Research in Ayurvedic Sciences (CCRAS)

(C) Central Council of Indian Medicine

(D) All of the above.

32. "Inspection Manual for inspection of Drug Testing Laboratories" has been published by

(A) Department of AYUSH

(B) Central Council for Research in Ayurvedic Sciences (CCRAS)

(C) Central Council of Indian Medicine

(D) All of the above.

33. "Good Clinical Practice Guidelines for clinical trials of ASU Medicine" has been published by

(A) Department of AYUSH

(B) Central Council for Research in Ayurvedic Sciences (CCRAS)

(C) Central Council of Indian Medicine

(D) Central Council of Unani Medicine.

34. "Guidelines for Inspection of GMP Compliance by ASU Drug Industry" has been published by

(A) Central Council for Research in Ayurvedic Sciences (CCRAS)

(B) Department of AYUSH

(C) Ministry of Family and Health Welfare

(D) Central Council of Siddha Medicine.

35. AYUSH-64 developed by Central Council for Research in Ayurvedic Sciences is used in the treatment of which of the following diseases?

(A) Malaria (B) Rheumatoid arthritis

(C) Typhoid fever (D) Typhus fever

36. AYUSH-SG developed by Central Council for Research in Ayurvedic Sciences is used in the treatment of which of the following diseases?

(A) Rheumatoid arthritis (B) Gout

(C) Ankylosing spondylitis (D) None of the above.

37. AYUSH-82 developed by Central Council for Research in Ayurvedic Sciences is used in the treatment of which of the following diseases?

(A) Diabetes mellitus (B) Diabetes insipidus

(C) Reactive hypoglycemia (D) Alimentary glycosuria.

38. List of Authoritative books of Ayurveda mentioned in First Schedule of Drugs & Cosmetic Act, 1940 is firmed by which of the following?

(A) Ayurveda Siddha Unani Drug Technical Advisory Board

(B) Ayurveda, Siddha, Unani Drugs Consultative Committee

(C) Indian Pharmacopoeial Commission

(D) Ministry of Family and Health Welfare

39. Pharmacopoeia Commission for Indian Medicine & Homoeopathy (PCIM&H) was initially established as

(A) Pharmacopoeia Commission for Indian Medicine

(B) Pharmacopoeia Commission for Ayurveda

(C) Pharmacopoeia Commission for AYUSH

(D) Pharmacopoeia Commission for ASU

40. Pharmacopoeia Commission for Indian Medicine & Homoeopathy serves as an umbrella organization for:

(A) Ayurvedic Pharmacopoeia Committee (APC)

(B) Siddha Pharmacopoeia Committee (SPC)

(C) Unani Pharmacopoeia Committee (UPC)

(D) Homoeopathic Pharmacopeia Committee (HPC).

(E) All of Above

41. Proof of effectiveness for new indication for granting license/approval to ASU medicine manufacturer is covered under which rule of Drug and Cosmetic Act?

(A) Section 33P (B) Rule 158-B
(C) Both of the above (D) None of the above

42. Nighantus in Ayurveda are classified on basis of which pattern?

(A) Pharmacopeial (B) Non-pharmacopeial
(C) Both of the above (D) Medicinal

43. Nirukt dravya in Ayurveda are addressed as:

(A) Pharmacopeial (B) Extrapharmacopeial
(C) Addendum (D) Formulary

44. Therapeutic is divided in to which of the following class?

(A) Rational (B) Empirical
(C) Non empirical (D) Rational and empirical

45. For the purpose of opening of Ayurvedic drug store obtaining license from state drug authority is:

(A) Mandatory (B) Non-mandatory
(C) Obligatory (D) None of the above

46. Under which central act, AYUSH pharmacists are registered?

(A) IMCC Act (B) HCC Act
(C) PCI Act (D) None of the above

47. Which of the following Nighantu is not included in authoritative books for Ayurveda as per Drug and Cosmetic Act?

(A) Bhavprakash (B) Dhanwantry
(C) Raj (D) Kaiydeva

48. Which of the following Nighantu is considered to be latest in classification of pharmacopeial type?

(A) Sodhala (B) Shaligram
(C) Madanpala (D) Rajvallabha

49. Pharmacopeial Laboratory of Indian Medicine (PLIM) is situated in which of the following cities?

(A) Ghaziabad (B) Nagpur

(C) Jalandhar (D) Kolkata.

50. Herbal Health Research Consortium is situated in which of the following cities of Punjab?

(A) Amritsar (B) Mohali

(C) Patiala (D) Ludhiana.

51. Central Council for Research in Ayurvedic Sciences has issued which of the following performa for disease cure claim?

(A) Drug claim (B) Disease claim

(C) Specific disease claim (D) All of the above.

52. Technical person for the purpose of Ayurvedic drug manufacturing unit should have which of the following qualifications as per Drug and Cosmetic Act?

(A) B.A.M.S (B) B. Pharm

(C) B.Sc (D) All of the above.

53. Which of the following performa is filled along with Form 24-D?

(A) Clinical trial (B) Disease claim

(C) Drug claim (D) None of the above.

54. AYUSH Standard awards quality seal to Ayurveda Siddha Unani (ASU) products for moving in which of the following markets?

(A) Domestic (B) International

(C) State (D) State capital.

55. AYUSH Premium Mark awards quality seal to Ayurveda Siddha Unani (ASU) products for moving in which of the following markets?

(A) Domestic (B) International

(C) State (D) International

56. Which of the following Voluntary Certification Scheme for AYUSH Products has been initiated by AYUSH in connection with Quality Council of India?

(A) AYUSH Standard (B) AYUSH Premium Mark

(C) Both of the above (D) None of the above.

57. Which of the following is scheme owner for Voluntary Certification Scheme for AYUSH Products?

(A) Department of AYUSH

(B) Quality Council of India

(C) Central Council of Indian Medicine

(D) All of the above.

58. Which of the following is manager for Voluntary Certification Scheme for AYUSH Products?

(A) Quality Council of India

(B) Department of AYUSH

(C) Central Council of Indian Medicine

(D) Ministry of Health and Family Welfare.

59. Which of the following body grant Certificate of Pharmaceutical Products (COPP) for Ayurvedic products?

(A) Central Drugs Standard Control Organization

(B) Quality Council of India

(C) Department of AYUSH

(D) None of the above.

60. Which of the following works for stopping and preventing publicity and advertisement of AYUSH related claims?

(A) Central Council of Indian Medicine

(B) The Advertising Standards Council Of India

(C) Department of AYUSH

(D) None of the above.

61. The qualification included in which of the following schedules is eligible for the purpose of teaching in Ayurvedic colleges?

(A) 1st schedule (B) 2nd schedule

(C) 3rd schedule (D) 4th schedule

62. Which of the following connect bring onboard all AYUSH facilities including hospitals and laboratories?

(A) AYUSH Grid

(B) AYUSH Research Portal

(C) AYUSH Drug Cell

(D) AYUSH Hospital Information Management System

63. Which portal deals with standard terminologies in AYUSH systems of medicine?

(A) National AYUSH Morbidity and Standardized Terminologies Electronic Portal

(B) AYUSH Research Portal

(C) AYUSH Hospital Information Management System

(D) Annotated Bibliography of Indian Medicine

64. The primary objective of the one of the following is to deal with the provisions of the Drugs and Cosmetics Act, 1940 and associated matters related to (ASU&H) drugs?

(A) AYUSH Drug Control Cell

(B) Central Council for Research in Ayurvedic Sciences

(C) Department of AYUSH

(D) Ayurveda, Siddha, Unani Drugs Technical Advisory Board (ASUDTAB)

65. Central Drugs Standard Control Organization categorize AYUSH drugs under?

(A) Traditional Medicine

(B) Alternative Medicine

(C) Herbal Medicine

(D) Ethnomedicine

66. The mandate of one of the following is to provide cost effective AYUSH Services, strengthen institutional capacity and support cultivation of medicinal plants?

(A) National AYUSH Mission

(B) AYUSH Drug Control Cell

(C) AYUSH Grid

(D) Department of AYUSH

67. Journal of Drug Research in Ayurvedic Sciences, Journal of Research in Ayurvedic Sciences and Journal of Indian Medical Heritage are published by one of the following?

(A) Central Council for Research in Ayurvedic Sciences

(B) Department of AYUSH

(C) Pharmacopeial Laboratory of Indian Medicine

(D) Central Council of Indian Medicine

68. The bill dealing with replacement of Central Council for Indian Medicine with a National Commission of Indian Medicine is known as?

(A) Indian Medical Central Council (IMCC) Act of 1970

(B) National Commission for Indian Systems of Medicine (NCISM) Bill

(C) The Indian Medicine and Homoeopathy Pharmacy Central Council Bill, 2016

(D) All of the above

69. Which application form is used for grant/renewal of a license to manufactures for sale of Ayurvedic/Siddha & Unani Drugs?

(A) Form 24-D (B) Form 24-E

(C) Both of the above (D) None of the above

70. Application form for grant/renewal of a Loan License to manufactures for sale of Ayurvedic/Siddha and Unani Drugs is which of the following?

(A) Form 24-D (B) Form 24-E

(C) Form 49 (D) None of the above

71. Which of the following system of medicine is not recognized in India?

(A) Alternative Medicine (B) Complementary Medicine

(C) Integrative Medicine (D) All of the above

72. Which of the following requires license for Ayurvedic drug manufacturing?

(A) Self Manufacturing (B) Loan Manufacturing

(C) Third-party manufacturing (D) All of the above

73. Which schedule of Drug & Cosmetic Act, 1945 describes fees for the test or analysis by the pharmacopoeial laboratory for Indian medicine (PLIM) or the government analyst?

(A) Schedule A (B) Schedule B

(C) Schedule B1 (D) Schedule D

74. Which schedule of Drug & Cosmetic Act, 1945 describes the List of poisonous substances under the Ayurvedic (including Siddha) and Unani Systems of Medicine?

(A) Schedule A (B) Schedule B

(C) Schedule D (D) Schedule E1

75. Which schedule of Drug & Cosmetic Act, 1945 describes the good manufacturing practices for Ayurvedic, Siddha and Unani medicines?

(A) Schedule A (B) Schedule D

(C) Schedule T (D) None of the above

76. Which schedule of Drug & Cosmetic Act, 1945 describes form for record of utilization of raw material by Ayurvedic, Siddha and Unani licensed manufacturing units during the financial year?

(A) Schedule T (B) Schedule TA

(C) Both of the above (D) None of the above

77. Which revised schedule of Drug & Cosmetic Act, 1945 has been opposed by the industry on ASU drugs?

(A) Schedule T

(B) Schedule Z

(C) Schedule D

(D) Schedule A

78. Clinical trials being conducted in the purview of the Department of AYUSH are to be registered with which of the following before enrollment of the first participant?

(A) The Clinical Trials Registry- India

(B) The Central Drugs Standard Control Organization

(C) Medical Council of India

(D) Central Council for Research in Ayurvedic Sciences

79. Which of the following publications have been pioneered by Central Council for Research in Ayurvedic Sciences?

(A) Phytochemistry, Drug Standardization and Quality Assurance

(B) Medico-Historical Studies and Literary Research

(C) Medicinal Plants Research

(D) All of the above

80. Health care Outreach Activities of Central Council for Research in Ayurvedic Sciences includes which of the following?

(A) Tribal Health Care Research Programme

(B) Ayurveda Mobile Health Care Programme under Scheduled Castes Sub Plan

(C) Integration of AYUSH (Ayurveda) with National Programme for prevention and Control of Cancer, Diabetes, Cardio-vascular disease and Stroke

(D) All of the above

81. Lifestyle and Dietary Advocacy Series pioneered by Central Council for Research in Ayurvedic Sciences includes which of the following?

(A) Ayurveda Based Diet and Life Style Guidelines for Prevention of Cardiac Disorders

(B) Ayurveda based diet & life Style Guidelines for Prevention and Management of Skin Diseases

(C) Ayurveda-Based Dietary Guidelines for Mental Disorders

(D) All of the above

82. For procurement of Ayurvedic Drugs in Central Government Health Scheme (CGHS) which of the following modes is allowed?

(A) Procurement without inviting tenders/rate enquiry

(B) Procurement by inviting tenders/rate enquiry

(C) Procurement through local purchase system

(D) All of the above.

83. In case of procurement without inviting tenders/rate enquiry in Central Government Health Scheme (CGHS), drugs and medicines should be manufactured by which of the following?

(A) Indian Medicines Pharmaceutical Corporation Limited

(B) Central Council for Research in Ayurvedic Sciences

(C) Department of AYUSH

(D) None of the above.

84. Which of the following has administrative control over Indian Medicines Pharmaceutical Corporation Limited?

(A) Department of AYUSH

(B) Central Council for Research in Ayurvedic Sciences

(C) Ministry of Health and Family Welfare

(D) Central Council of Indian Medicine.

85. In case of procurement by inviting tenders/rate enquiry in Central Government Health Scheme (CGHS), drugs and medicines can be procured from which of the following?

(A) Open market

(B) Indian Medicines Pharmaceutical Corporation Limited

(C) Both of the above

(D) None of the above.

86. In case of procurement through local purchase system in Central Government Health Scheme (CGHS), drugs and medicines can be procured from which of the following?

(A) Open market

(B) Indian Medicines Pharmaceutical Corporation Limited

(C) Approved local chemist

(D) (A) and (B).

87. Under Central Government Health Scheme (CGHS), formularies of Ayurvedic Medicines fall in which of the following?

(A) Formulary for medicines manufactured by Indian Medicines Pharmaceutical Corporation Limited

(B) Formulary for medicines not manufactured by Indian Medicines Pharmaceutical Corporation Limited

(C) Non formulary medicines

(D) (A) and (B).

88. Under the Central Government Health Scheme (CGHS), drugs provided by Indian Medicines Pharmaceutical Corporation Limited should have

(A) Barcode

(B) ASU License

(C) Loan license

(D) Certificate of analysis.

89. Under the Central Government Health Scheme, non formulary medicines are included in which of the following categories?

(A) Formulary for medicines manufactured by Indian Medicines Pharmaceutical Corporation Limited

(B) Formulary for medicines not manufactured by Indian Medicines Pharmaceutical Corporation Limited

(C) Prescribed the physicians

(D) Ayurvedic Formulary of India.

90. Publication named "Accreditation Standards for Panchkarma Clinics" has been pioneered by which of the following?

(A) Quality Council of India

(B) National Accreditation Board for Hospitals and Healthcare Providers

(C) National Accreditation Board for Laboratories

(D) Department of AYUSH.

91. AYUSH Health & Wellness Centres are being established by Ministry of AYUSH under Ayushman Bharat scheme, through State/UT Governments within which of the following?

(A) Centrally Sponsored Scheme of National AYUSH Mission

(B) National Health Mission (NHM)

(C) AYUSH Grid

(D) National Health Policy.

92. Medical facility under ECHS for AYUSH systems of medicine can be availed at which of the following:

(A) Government AYUSH hospital & colleges/National Institute of AYUSH

(B) Government dispensaries/district hospitals

(C) Municipality hospitals

(D) All of the above.

93. How many volumes of Ayurvedic Pharmacopoeia of India for single drugs have been published so far?

(A) 5 (B) 7

(C) 8 (D) 9

94. Information on Hydro-alcoholic & Water extracts of drugs used in Ayurveda have been provided in which volume (s) of Ayurvedic Pharmacopoeia of India?

(A) 8 (B) 9

(C) Both of the above (D) All volumes.

95. How many volumes of Ayurvedic Pharmacopoeia of India for formulations have been published so far?

(A) 2 (B) 3

(C) 4 (D) None of the above.

96. How many parts of Ayurvedic Formulary of India have been published so far?

(A) 2 (B) 1

(C) 3 (D) None of the above.

97. Supporting Pharmacopoeial Publications for Ayurveda pioneered by Pharmacopoeia Commission for Indian Medicine & Homoeopathy (PCIM&H) includes?

(A) Thin Layer Chromatography (TLC) Atlas

(B) Macroscopy and Microscopy Atlas

(C) Both of the above

(D) None of the above

98. The schemes funded by the Department of AYUSH fall under which category?

(A) Central Sector Scheme

(B) Centrally Sponsored Schemes

(C) Extra Mural Research

(D) All of the above.

99. CCRAS has formulated guidelines for Ayurvedic Practitioners for Clinical Management of which of the following diseases?

(A) Dengue and Chikungunya

(B) Nipah Virus

(C) Covid 19

(D) All of the above

100. Mechanism to support short-term research projects for evaluating the impact of AYUSH interventions cum medicines in the prophylaxis and clinical management of COVID-19 falls under which scheme?

(A) Extramural Scheme

(B) Modified Extramural Scheme

(C) Central Sector Scheme

(D) Centrally Sponsored Schemes

101. Which of the following titles have been pioneered by the Medicinal Plant Division of Indian Council of Medical Research (ICMR)?

(A) Quality Standard of Indian Medicinal Plants

(B) Reviews on Indian Medicinal Plants

(C) Ayurvedic Pharmacopoeia of India

(D) (A) and (B)

102. ICMR-National Institute of Traditional Medicine (NITM) is located in which State of India?

(A) Kerala (B) Karnataka

(C) Tamilnadu (D) Orissa

103. The first schedule of Drug and Cosmetic Act, includes authoritative books for which of the following?

(A) Ayurveda (B) Siddha

(C) Unani Tibb (D) All of the above.

104. The first schedule of Drug and Cosmetic Act deals with one of the following aspect of ASU drugs?

(A) Standards of drugs (B) Quality control

(C) Quality assurance (D) Agrotechniques

105. The emerging discipline based on herbal extracts is known as?

(A) Phytopharmaceuticals (B) Herbal Medicine

(C) Phytotherapy (D) Phytomedicine

106. Extracts can be compared with which of the following Ayurvedic pharmacopoeial preparation?

(A) Ghansatva (B) Gutika

(C) Vati (D) Aristha

107. Which of the following phytochemical is considered to be nephrotoxic?

(A) Aristolochic acid (B) Hippuruic acid

(C) Fulvic acid (D) Aconitic acid

108. Decoction (kwath or kadha) advocated by AYUSH Ministry for immunity booster measure does not contain one of the following?

(A) Guduchi (B) Sunthi

(C) Tulsi (D) Tvak

109. What is the amount of turmeric used in the preparation of golden milk?

(A) ½ teaspoonful (B) 1 teaspoonful

(C) 2 teaspoonful (D) None of the above.

110. Ayushman-8 developed by Central Council for Research in Ayurvedic Sciences is used in the treatment of which of the following diseases?

(A) Mental retardation (B) Epilepsy

(C) Hysteria (D) Schizophrenia.

111. Coded drug AYUSH QOL-2C developed by Central Council for Research in Ayurvedic Sciences is used in improving quality of life of patients suffering from?

(A) Cancer (B) Diabetes mellitus

(C) Hepatitis (D) Cirrhosis

112. As per Department of AYUSH standard definition of AYUSH is which one of the following?

(A) Complementary and Alternative System

(B) Integrative Medicine

(C) Traditional and Non-Conventional Systems of Healthcare

(D) Alternative Medicine

113. The decoction (kwath) recommended by Department of AYUSH can be sold under which of the following generic names?

(A) AYUSH Kwath (B) AYUSH Kudineer

(C) AYUSH Joshanda (D) All of the above.

114. AYUSH Rasayan A & B developed by Central Council for Research in Ayurvedic Sciences is used in which of the following?

(A) Geriatric health (B) Macular denegation

(C) Senile dementia (D) Osterarthrosis.

115. AYUSH C1 Oil developed by Central Council for Research in Ayurvedic Sciences is used in which of the following?

(A) Wound healing (B) Burn treatment

(C) Skin diseases (D) Rheumatism.

116. AYUSH PJ-7 Oil developed by Central Council for Research in Ayurvedic Sciences is used in which of the following diseases?

(A) Chikungunya (B) Dengue

(D) Nipah (D) Swine

117. AYUSH M-3 developed by Central Council for Research in Ayurvedic Sciences is used in which of the following diseases?

(A) Migraine (B) Scalp mylagia

(C) Frontal sinusitis (D) None of the above.

118. AYUSH SL developed by Central Council for Research in Ayurvedic Sciences is used in which of the following diseases?

(A) Filariasis (B) Guinea worm

(C) Hookworm (D) Tapeworm

119. AYUSH A developed by Central Council for Research in Ayurvedic Sciences is used in which of the following diseases?

(A) Bronchial Asthma (B) Acute bronchitis

(C) Pneumonia (D) Chronic bronchitis

120. AYUSH D developed by Central Council for Research in Ayurvedic Sciences is used in which of the following diseases?

(A) Bronchial Asthma (B) Diabetes mellitus

(C) Diabetes insipidus (D) Albuminuria

121. Carctol S developed by Central Council for Research in Ayurvedic Sciences is used in which of the following diseases?

(A) Cancer (B) AIDS

(C) Hepatitis (D) Rheumatoid arthritis

122. AYUSH K1 developed by Central Council for Research in Ayurvedic Sciences is used in which of the following diseases?

(A) Chronic Kidney Diseases (B) Nephrolithiasis

(C) Heart diseases (D) Liver diseases

123. Central Council for Research in Ayurvedic Sciences has signed Memorandum of Understanding (MoU) for undertaking collaboration, research and clinical studies with which of the following universities?

(A) Banaras Hindu University

(B) Gujarat Ayurved University

(C) Utkal University

(D) Guru Ravi Das Ayurved University.

124. For which disease, Central Council for Research in Ayurvedic Sciences initiated work on Parijata Ghana Vati?

(A) Malaria (B) Tuberculosis

(C) AIDS (D) Hepatitis

125. Ayush 64 for malaria, Ayush SG for Rheumatoid Arthritis, Ayush 82 for Diabetes mellitus have been developed and commercialized through

(A) National Productivity Council

(B) National Research Development Corporation

(C) None of the above

(D) Both of the above.

126. AYUSH 64 has been recently selected for clinical trial in which of the following disease?

(A) COVID 19 (B) SARS

(C) Nipah (D) H1N1

127. Which chemical constituent present in *Withania somnifera* has been tested for efficacy against COVID 19?

(A) Withaferin A (B) Withanone

(C) Cuscohygrine (D) Anahygrine

128. Is it mandatory to register AYUSH clinic under Clinical Establishment Act?

(A) No (B) Yes

(C) None of the above (D) Both of the above.

129. Amchi system of Medicine is also known as

(A) Sowa-Rigpa (B) Tibetan System of Medicine

(C) Both of the above (D) None of the above.

130. Is Amchi system of Medicine recognized by Central Council of Indian Medicine for the purpose of teaching and practice?

(A) Yes (B) No

(C) Derecognized (D) None of the above.

131. The methodology adopted in Development of Minimum Standards of Clinical Establishments for Ayurveda is based on which of the following?

(A) Central Council of Indian Medicine norms

(B) Indian Public Health Standards Guidelines

(C) Minimum Standard Regulations for Ayurvedic hospitals in Gujarat.

(D) All of the above.

132. Under IMCC Act 1970 what is the status of registered Vaidyas, Siddhas and Hakeems preparing medicines on their own to dispense to their patients and not selling such drugs in the market?

(A) Permitted (B) Exempted

(C) Both of the above (D) None of (A) and (B).

133. Quality control section for AYUSH having microbiologist should have at least which of the following qualifications?

(A) Bachelor degree

(B) Master degree

(C) Doctorate

(D) Postgraduate diploma.

134. Quality control section for AYUSH having chemist should have at least which of the following qualifications?

(A) Master Degree in Science

(B) Master Degree in Pharmacy

(C) Master Degree in Pharmacy (Ayurveda)

(D) All of the above.

135. Quality control section for AYUSH having Botanist or Pharmacognosist should have at least which of the following qualifications?

(A) Bachelor Degree in Science (Medical)

(B) Bachelor Degree in Pharmacy (Ayurveda)

(C) Master Degree in Science (Medical)

(D) (A) and (B).

136. B.A.M.S degree Qualification Required for Ayurvedic Medicine Manufacturing should be conferred by which of the following?

(A) University

(B) A State Government or Statutory Faculties

(C) Councils and Boards of Indian Systems of Medicine

(D) All of the above.

137. Qualification Required for Ayurvedic Medicine Manufacturing should be conferred by which of the following?

(A) University

(B) A State Government or Statutory Faculties

(C) Councils and Boards of Indian Systems of Medicine

(D) All of the above.

138. A graduate in Pharmacy or Pharmaceutical Chemistry or Chemistry or Botany of a University recognized by the Central Government should have how many years of experience in ASU drug manufacturing?

(A) 1 (B) 2

(C) 3 (D) 5.

139. A Vaid or Hakim registered in a State Register of Practitioners of indigenous systems of medicines should have how many years of experience in ASU drug manufacturing?

(A) 4 (B) 2

(C) 1 (D) 5

140. A qualification as Pharmacist in Ayurvedic (including Siddha) or Unani systems of medicine should have how many years of experience in ASU drug manufacturing recognized by the Central Government?

(A) 8 (C) 6

(C) 5 (D) 1

141. Which of the following AYUSH University is awarding PhD in Phytochemistry?

(A) Rajasthan Ayurved University

(B) Uttrakhand Ayurved University

(C) Banaras Hindu University

(D) Guru Ravi Das Ayurved University.

142. Which of the following are subtypes of Proprietary ASU Formulations?

(A) Medicinal formulation

(B) Nutritive Formulation

(C) Cosmaceutical Formulation

(D) Aqueous or Hydro alcoholic Extract based Formulation

(E) All of the above.

143. License requirements for Classical/Shastriya Formulations includes

(A) Shastriya ASU formulation with dosage form and indications as per authoritative text

(B) Shastriya ASU formulation with change in dosage form

(C) Shastriya ASU formulation with new indication

(D) All of the above.

144. License Requirements for Proprietary Formulations includes

(A) Proprietary formulation with ingredients not from Schedule E(I) and based on textual rationale from authoritative books

(B) Proprietary formulation with any of the ingredients from Schedule E (I) and based on textual rationale from authoritative books.

(C) Both of the above

(D) None of the above.

145. The emerging subject Phtyopharmaceuticals is under the purview of which of the following departments?

(A) Department of AYUSH

(B) Central Drugs Standard Control Organization

(C) Indian Council of Medical Research

(D) Department of Health Research.

146. Under the phytopharmaceutical concept, how many markers are required to be proved in the purified extract?

(A) 1 (B) 2

(C) 3 (D) 4

147. Which of the following Homeopathic remedy has been advocated by Department of AYUSH in COVID 19?

(A) Arsenicum album 30 (B) Calphos

(C) Nux vomica (D) All of the above.

148. Central Sector Scheme of National Medicinal Plant Board is related to which of the following?

(A) Conservation (B) Herbal Garden

(C) Marketing and trade (D) All of the above.

149. Voluntary Certification Scheme for Medicinal Plant Produce (VCSMPP) is maintained under the aegis of which of the following?

(A) National Medicinal Plant Board

(B) Central Council for Research in Ayurvedic Sciences

(C) Department of AYUSH

(D) Central Council of Indian Medicine.

150. Regulatory affairs related to AYUSH or ASU drugs are under the purview of which of the following?

(A) Department of AYUSH

(B) Sate Drug License Authority

(C) Central Council for Research in Ayurvedic Sciences

(D) Both (A) and (B).

151. Research Database on Ayurveda, Siddha, Other Traditional Medicine and Related Sciences Part- I, II, III & IV have been published by which of the following organizations?

(A) Central Council for Research in Ayurvedic Sciences

(B) Department of AYUSH

(C) Central Council of Indian Medicine

(D) None of the above.

152. Pharmacognosy of Indigenous Drugs Volume I, II & III have been published by which of the following organizations?

(A) Department of AYUSH

(B) Central Council of Indian Medicine

(C) Central Council for Research in Ayurvedic Sciences

(D) National Medicinal Plant Board

153. Which of the following provides suggestions/inputs related to planning/designing /protocol related, sampling and statistical issues etc. as required by M.D./M.S, Ph.D scholars and guides across Ayurvedic Institutes/Colleges?

(A) AYUSH Research Portal

(B) Research Management Information System

(C) Annotated Bibliography of Indian Medicine

(D) All of the above.

154. e-*Nighantu* (Collection of *Ayurvedic* Lexicons) is the project initialed by which of the following organizations?

(A) National Institute of Medical Heritage

(B) National Medicinal Plant Board

(C) Gujarat Ayurved University

(D) None of the above.

155. SCHEDULE–E (I): List of Poisonous Substances under the Ayurvedic Medicine deals with which of the following?

(A) Drugs of vegetable origin

(B) Drugs of animal origin

(C) Drugs of mineral origin

(D) All of the above.

156. AYUSH products are classified broadly in which of the following groups?

(A) ASU classical products

(B) ASU foods

(C) ASU cosmetics

(D) Ethically promoted and OTC products

(E) All of the above.

157. Legally speaking AYUSH products can be divided into which of the following categories?

(A) Classical products

(B) Proprietary medicines

(C) Both of the above

(D) None of the above.

158. Maximum content of alcohol (w/w) allowed for 30 ml size of packing for *Mrtsanjivanisura* is?

(A) 10% (B) 12%

(C) 14% (D) 16%.

159. Maximum content of alcohol (w/w) allowed for 120 ml size of packing for *Mahadraksasava* is?

(A) 10% (B) 12%

(C) 14% (D) 16%.

160. Which of the following Sub-Committees are functioning under Ayurvedic Pharmacopoeia Committee?

(A) Formulary Sub-Committee

(B) Ayurveda Single Drugs Sub-Committee

(C) Sub-Committee of Pharmacogonosy

(D) Sub-Committee of Photochemistry & Chemistry.

(E) All of the above.

161. Traditional Knowledge Digital Library is a collaborative project poinered by which of the following?

(A) Council of Scientific and Industrial Research

(B) Ministry of Science and Technology

(C) Department of AYUSH

(D) All of the above

162. *Kamini Vidrawan Ras* is mentioned in which of the following texts?

(A) Ayurveda Saar Sangreh

(B) Bhaishajya Ratnavali

(C) Ayurvedic Formulary of India

(D) (A) and (B)

163. Golden Triangle Partnership (GTP) Scheme is aimed at which of the following?

(A) Validation of traditional Ayurvedic Drugs

(B) Toxicology of Ayurvedic Drugs

(C) Ethnopharmacology

(D) Quality assurance

164. The departments involved in execution of mandate of Golden Triangle Partnership (GTP) are which from the following?

(A) Department of AYUSH

(B) Indian Council of Medical Research

(C) Council of Scientific and Industrial Research

(D) All of the above.

165. Tribal pockets of Nilgiris-Recording of the field study on medical flora and health practices named monograph has been published by which one of the following?

(A) Department of AYUSH

(B) Central Council of Research in Ayurvedic Sciences or Central Council for Research in Indian Medicine and Homeopathy

(C) Division of Medicinal Plants, Indian Council of Medical Sciences

(D) Central Council of Indian Medicine.

166. Can Ayurveda medicines be sold through Pradhan Mantri Bharatiya Jan Aushadhi Pariyojana?

(A) Yes

(B) No

(C) Under process

(D) None of the above.

167. Institute of Teaching and Research in Ayurveda Bill, 2020 introduced in Parliament for the establishment of an Institute of Teaching and Research in Ayurveda in which of the following cities?

(A) Jamnagar

(B) Jaipur

(C) Delhi

(D) Patna.

168. AIMIL Pharma has developed anti-diabetes medicine under brand name BGR-34 in association with which of the following?

(A) Council of Scientific and Industrial Research

(B) Division of Medicinal Plants, Indian Council of Medical Sciences

(C) Central Council of Research in Ayurvedic Sciences

(D) Central Council of Indian Medicine.

169. Central Sector Scheme of Pharmacovigilance of Ayurvedic, Siddha, Unani and Homoeopathic drugs involves which of the following?

(A) Peripheral Pharmacovigilance Centers

(B) Intermediary Pharmacovigilance Centers

(C) National Pharmacovigilance Co-ordination Centre

(D) All of the above.

170. AYUSH-UT Ointment developed by Central Council of Research in Ayurvedic Sciences is indicated in the treatment of which disease?

(A) Vulvo vaginitis (B) Dyspareunia

(C) Both of the above (D) None of the above.

171. AYUSH-KD Ointment developed by Central Council of Research in Ayurvedic Sciences is indicated in the treatment of which disease?

(A) Trichomoniasis (B) Vulvo vaginitis

(C) General vaginitis (D) All of the above.

172. AYUSH-KVM Syrup developed by Central Council of Research in Ayurvedic Sciences is indicated in the treatment of which disease?

(A) Cough and cold (B) Acute bronchitis

(C) Chronic bronchitis (D) Bronchial asthma.

173. AYUSH-VRG Tablet developed by Central Council of Research in Ayurvedic Sciences is indicated in the treatment of which disease?

(A) Primary dysmenorrhoea

(B) Secondary dysmenorrhoea

(C) Menorrhagia

(D) Metrorrgahia.

174. AYUSH-VRG Tablet developed by Central Council of Research in Ayurvedic Sciences is indicated in the treatment of which disease?

(A) Primary dysmenorrhoea (B) Secondary dysmenorrhoea

(C) Menorrhagia (D) *Metrorrhagia.*

175. AYUSH-LND Tablet developed by Central Council of Research in Ayurvedic Sciences is indicated in the treatment of which disease?

(A) Primary dysmenorrhoea

(B) Secondary dysmenorrhoea

(C) Dysfunctional uterine bleeding

(D) *Metrorrhagia.*

176. Which of the following institute has been designated as National Pharmacovigilance Centre?

(A) All India Institute of Ayurveda, New Delhi

(B) Gujarat Ayurved University

(C) National Institute of Ayurveda, Jaipur

(D) All of the above.

177. The statement that validity of GMP Certificate has been extended to five years from 3 years is

(A) Correct (B) Partially correct

(C) Incorrect (D) Under process.

178. The Central Government created the Department of ISM&H in which year?

(A) 1991 (B) 1992

(C) 1994 (D) 1995.

179. AYUSH-57 is used in the treatment of whcich skin disease?

(A) Leucoderma (B) Scabies

(C) Psoriasis (D) Pemphigus.

180. AYUSH-64 has been investigated for utility in which of the following diseases?

(A) Rhinovirus

(B) Respiratory syncytial *v*irus

(C) Influenza-like illness

(D) Polio virus.

181. The clinical efficacy of AYUSH-64 has been investigated in which of the following diseases?

(A) Malaria (B) Filaria

(C) Influenza-like illness (D) All of the above.

182. Which of the following *bhasma* has been found to less toxic in experimental studies?

(A) *Tamra Bhasma* (B) *Somnathi Tamra Bhasma*

(C) Both of the above (D) None of the above.

183. Which of the following committees are working for implementation of AYUSH Pharmacovigilance Programme?

(A) Steering and Monitoring Committee

(B) Technical Advisory Committee

(C) Central Signal Detection & Causality Assessment Committee

(D) All of the above.

184. AYUSH clinical expert and Pharmacy expert of AYUSH system are part of which of the following committees working for implementation of AYUSH Pharmacovigilance Programme?

(A) Steering and Monitoring Committee

(B) Technical Advisory Committee

(C) Central Signal Detection & Causality Assessment Committee

(D) None of the above.

185. Pharmacology expert from AIIMS/ ICMR and Representative from CDSCO are part of which of the following committees working for implementation of AYUSH Pharmacovigilance Programme?

(A) Steering and Monitoring Committee

(B) Technical Advisory Committee

(C) Central Signal Detection & Causality Assessment Committee

(D) None of the above.

186. Cod-liver oil contains which of the following ingredients?

(A) Vitamin A & B

(B) Macro & micronutrients

(C) Fatty acid, resin & cholesterol

(D) All of the above.

187. Fill in the blank from following that the vitamin content of Halibut liver oil is ----------------------as compared to Cod-liver oil?

(A) More (B) Less

(C) Superior (D) Inferior.

188. The elemental calcium content of cuttlefish (*Samdurphena*) is

(A) 80-85% (B) 90-95%

(C) 98% (D) 100%.

189. The publication 'Clinical Trials on AYUSH Interventions for COVID-19: Methodology and Protocol Development' has been carried out by which of the following?

(A) Interdisciplinary AYUSH Research and Development Task Force Ministry of AYUSH

(B) Gujarat Ayurved University

(C) National Institute of Ayurveda, Jaipur

(D) None of the above.

190. In physicochemical analysis of *Samaguna Rasasindur* % of mercury has been reported as one of the following?

(A) 83.68% (B) 85%

(C) 90% (D) 98%.

191. Which of the element has been detected in *Shadguna Balijarita Makaradhwaja* by inductively coupled plasma optical emission spectrometry study?

(A) Zinc (B) Gold

(C) Mercury (D) Sulphur.

192. In physicochemical analysis of *Shadaguna gandhaka jarita Rasasindur* % of mercury has been reported as one of the following?

(A) 81.93% (B) 85%

(C) 90% (D) 98%.

193. Which of the following has been suggested as marker compound for the purpose of quality control in *Lohasava* and *Pippalyasava*?

(A) Ellagic acid (B) Gallic acid

(C) Tannic acid (D) Pyrogallic acid.

194. The percentage of alcohol generation after fermentation of traditionally prepared *Arjunarishta* has been reported as

(A) 5.94%w/w (B) 6.42%w/w

(C) 7.30%w/w (D) None of the above.

195. Which of the following have been quantified in *Arjunarishta* by validated HPTLC densitometry?

(A) Ellagic acid

(B) Gallic acid

(C) Tannic acid

(D) Ellagic acid & Gallic acid.

196. Rat studies have demonstrated which of the following activity of *Triguna Makaradhwaja*?

(A) Immunomodulator

(B) Immunosuppresant

(C) Diseases modifying anti rheumatic

(D) Cardioprotective.

197. *Drakshasava* can be differentiated from *Draksharishta* on basis of which of the following parameters?

(A) pH

(B) Reducing and non-reducing sugar

(C) Alcohol

(D) All of the above.

198. The alcoholic content of *Karpurasava* has been reported to be which of the following?

(A) 8.7% (B) 9.7%

(C) 10.7% (D) None of the above.

199. The alcoholic content of *Aswagandhadyarishta* has been reported to be which of the following?

(A) 6.9% (B) 7.1%

(C) 10.7% (D) None of the above.

200. The alcoholic content of *Asokarishta* has been reported to be which of the following?

(A) 4.68% (B) 7.1%

(C) 10.7% (D) None of the above.

201. The percentage of tin in *Vangabhasma* has been reported to be which of the following?

(A) 56.00% (B) 66.43%

(C) 70.89% (D) None of the above.

202. With regard to toxicity studies in case of *Swarna–Vanga*, which of the following is correct?

(A) Non toxic (B) Moderately toxic

(C) Toxic (D) None of the above.

203. In case of Conch shell (*Shankha*), after calcinations (*Shankha Bhasma*) calcium carbonate present in aragonite form gets converted into which form?

(A) Calcite (B) Vatrite

(C) Both of the above (D) None of the above.

204. In case of Coveries (*Kapardi*), after calcinations (*Kapardi Bhasma*) calcium carbonate present in aragonite form gets converted into which form?

(A) Calcite (B) Vatrite

(C) Both of the above (D) None of the above.

205. A study has proved presence of which of the following compounds in *Rasa Parpati*?

(A) Mercuric sulfide (B) Mercuric oxide

(C) Mixture of both (D) None of the above.

206. What amount of aconitine has been proved in the periodical analysis of *Tribhuwan Kirti Rasa*?

(A) 0.026% (B) 0.028%

(C) 0.030% (D) 0.032%.

207. Which of the following are estimated in *Triphala Churna* by visible spectrophotometric method?

(A) Alkaloids (B) Simple tannins

(C) Hydrolysable tannins (D) Glycosides.

208. Which of the following is estimated as a marker compound in *Ajmodadi churna*?

(A) Gallic acid (B) Piperine

(C) Fixed oil (D) Flavonoids.

209. Based on the stability study and on basis of total tannins, the shelf-life of *Triphala churna* is which one of the following?

(A) Short (B) Very short

(C) Long (D) Very long.

210. Which of the following has been suggested as a marker compound for *Triphala churna*?

(A) Gallic acid (B) Piperine

(C) Fixed oil (D) Flavonoids.

211. Major chemical constituents present in *Kshiramandura* are which one of the following?

(A) Ferric oxide (B) Magnesium carbonate

(C) Calcium carbonate oil (D) All of above.

212. Major chemical constituents present in *Mandura bhasma* are which one of the following?

(A) Ferric oxide (B) Silicon dioxide

(C) Both (A) and (B) (D) All of above.

213. The major chemical constituents present in *Kumaryasava* are which one of the following?

(A) Alkaloids (B) Anthraquinones

(C) Glycosides (D) All of above.

214. Which of the following mentioned method has been employed for standardization of *Chandraprabha vati*?

(A) HPLC (B) HPTLC

(C) Colorimetric (D) GC-MS.

215. *Shevtaparpati* is also addressed by which of the following names?

(A) *Gaganparpati* (B) *Bolaparpati*

(C) *Ksharaparpati* (D) *Rasaparpati*

216. Which of the following mentioned activity has been proved in favor of *Loha parpati*?

(A) Cardioprotective (B) Renoprotective

(C) Hepatoprotective (D) Neuroprotective.

217. A double blind study has reported efficacy of *Arogyavardhini* in Which of the following mentioned diseases?

(A) Acute viral hepatitis (B) Alcoholic hepatitis

(C) Chronic persistent jaundice (D) Biliary cirrhosis.

218. Efficacy of *Rasa Manikya* in the possible treatment of which of the following diseases has been reported?

(A) Gout (B) Rheumatic arthritis

(C) Rheumatoid arthritis (D) Psoriatic arthritis.

219. Which of the following formulation is indicated in the treatment of inflammation of the intestine?

(A) *Makardhwaj* (B) *Siddhmakardhwaj*

(C) *Rasa Puspha* (D) *Rasa Sindoor.*

220. Which of the following formulation is used for *rasayana* action?

(A) *Makardhwaj*

(B) *Siddhmakardhwaj (described in Bhaishajya Ratnavali)*

(C) *Siddhmakardhwaj (described in Rasa Tarangini)*

(D) None of the above.

221. *Makardhwaj* has which of the following properties?

(A) Rasayana (B) Vajikarna

(C) Both of the above (D) None of the above.

222. *Rasa Karpura* is also addressed by which of the following names?

(A) *Rasa manjari* (B) Perchloride of mercury.

(C) Both of the above (D) None of the above.

223. Which preparation of *Rasamanikya* has showed better results from the standardization point of view and quality assurance?

(A) *Abhraka patra method* (B) *Sharava samputa method*

(C) Fuse bulb method (D) None of the above.

224. The minimum and maximum percentage of arsenic present in *Samirpannaga Rasa* is which one from the following?

(A) 30.28-32.50%w/w (B) 32.28-32.70%w/w

(C) 40.28-42.50%w/w (D) None of the above.

225. The maximum amount of arsenic present in *Mal Sindoora* is which one from the following?

(A) 14.30%w/w (B) 16.30%w/w

(C) 18.30%w/w (D) 20.30%w/w

226. The minimum and maximum percentage of gold present in *Svaran Parpati* is which one from the following?

(A) 6.0-10.3%w/w (B) 8.0-10.3%w/w

(C) 10.0-10.3%w/w (D) None of the above.

227. Which of the following salts are present in *Svaran Vanga*?

(A) SnS_2 (B) SnO_2

(C) Both of the above (D) None of the above.

228. In experimental studies *Rasakarpura* has been shown to be safe in which of the following studies as compared to mercuric chloride?

(A) Acute (B) Sub acute

(C) Chronic (D) None of the above.

229. The amount of mercury in *Rajata Sindura* as confirmed by Scanning electron microscope coupled with energy dispersive spectroscopy analysis is which one of the following?

(A) 85.21% (B) 86.21%

(C) 87.21% (D) 88.21%

230. In experimental studies, which of the following activity has been studied for *Rajahpravartini vati*?

(A) Estrogenic (B) Antioestrogenic

(B) Both (D) None.

231. Which of the following constituents have been estimated in *Dashang lepa*?

(A) Phenolic (B) Flavonoid

(C) Alkaloid (D) Both (A) and (B).

232. Which of the following constituent has been estimated in *Kalyanavleha* by HPTLC?

(A) Allicin (B) Berberine

(C) Curcumin (D) Piperine.

233. In experimental studies, which of the following activity has been reported for *Sitopaladi churna*?

(A) Antiallergic (B) Anti tachyphylaxis

(C) Mast cell stabilizing (D) All of the above.

234. Percentage of gold found in *Swarna Bhasma* is which one of the following?

(A) 96.76%w/w (B) 98%w/w

(C) 99%w/w (D) 100%w/w.

235. Minimum and maximum silver detected in *Rajat Bhasma* is which one of the following?

(A) 52.57-59.39%w/w (B) 54.57-59.49%w/w

(C) 56.57-69.39%w/w (D) None of above.

236. Minimum and maximum percentage of tin as SnS_2 detected in *Vang Bhasma* is which one of the following?

(A) 63.74-81.40%w/w (B) 73.74-81.40%w/w

(C) 83.74-81.40%w/w (D) None of above.

237. Percentage of zinc as ZnO found in *Vang Bhasma* is which one of the following?

(A) 91.47%w/w (B) 93%w/w

(C) 99%w/w (D) 100%w/w.

238. Nephroprotective activity of which of the following formulation has been proved in experimental studies in oral sodium phosphate induced nephritis?

(A) *Tamra bhasma* (B) *Loha bhasma*

(C) *Vanga bhasma* (D) *Yasada bhasma.*

239. *Pushpadhanwa rasa* has demonstrated spermatogenic activity against which of the following medicinal plant induced infertility in animal studies?

(A) *Solanum nigrum* (B) *Solanum ferox*

(C) *Solanum indicum* (D) *Solanum xanthocaprum.*

240. Which of the following sterol compound is taken as standard for estimation of sterols in *Dashmulakwatha* by HPTLC?

(A) Campesterol (B) α-Spinasterol

(C) β-Sitosterol (D) alpha1-Sitosterol.

241. Clinical trial of which of the following formulation has been studied on female infertility?

(A) *Rajpravartini vati* (B) *Nashtapushpantak Ras*

(C) *Phalaghrita* (D) *Pushpadhanwa Ras.*

242. Which of the following formulation was used in the development of female contraceptive by CCRAS?

(A) *Ashokarista* (B) *Lodhrasva*

(C) *Pippalyadi yoga* (D) *Pushpadhanwa Ras.*

243. The efficacy of *Pushpadhanwa Ras* in the management of which of the following disease has been reported?

(A) Ovarian cancer (B) Polycystic ovarian disease

(C) Atrophic vaginitis (D) All of above.

244. Which of the following activities have been repotted in favor of Chandraprabha vati?

(A) Antidiabetic (B) Anti-inflammatory

(C) Hypoglycemic (D) All of above.

245. Under Collaborative Clinical Research, CCRAS has completed validation of C1-Oil in association with AIIMS for which of the following activity?

(A) Wound healing (B) Psoriasis

(C) Leucoderma (D) Lichen planus.

246. *Vyomashma pisthi* has which of the following actions?

(A) Heart tonic (B) Antihypertensive

(C) Both of above (D) None of above.

247. Which of the following pharmacopoeia dosage form of *Vyomashma* is used in medicine?

(A) Bhasma (B) Pishti

(C) Powder (D) Decoction.

248. Efficacy of *Dhatri loha* has been studied in the management of which type of anemia?

(A) Iron deficiency anemia (B) Megaloblastic anemia

(C) Pernicious anemia (D) All of above.

249. Diuretic activity of which of the formulation of coconut has been studied?

(A) Coconut husk *mashi* (B) *Narikela lavana*

(C) Coconut oil (D) All of above.

250. Which of the following formulation has been found to be useful in AIIDS?

(A) AC II (B) AYUSH 64

(C) *Shilajit rasayana* (D) None of above.

251. Which of the following formulation has been found to be useful in AIIDS?

(A) AC II (B) AYUSH 64

(C) *Shilajit rasayana* (D) None of above.

252. Which of the following *Pishti* has nootropic (intellect promoting) action?

(A) Gomeda (B) Vadurya

(C) Hiraka (D) (A) and (B).

253. Which of the following *Bhasma* has *yogvahi* (bioenhancer) action?

(A) Hiraka (B) Mukta

(C) Nilama (D) All of them.

254. Which of the following *Bhasma* is used in the treatment of alcoholism?

(A) Suryakant (B) Chandrakant

(C) Rajavarta (D) Parojak.

255. *Parojak Bhasma* is used in the treatment of which calls of poisoning?

(A) Sthavar (B) Jangham

(C) Gara (D) All of them.

256. Which of the following activity of *Kasisa bhasma* has been reported in patients undergoing elective surgery?

(A) Haematinic (B) Antihypertensive

(C) Cardioprotective (D) Antianginal.

257. Which of the following activity *of Muktashukti bhasma* has been reported in animal studies?

(A) *Anti-inflammatory* (B) Analgesic

(C) Antipyretic (D) Antianginal.

258. What level of alcohol has been tested during quality assessment of different marketed brands of *Dasmoolaristam?*

(A) Less than 12% v/v (B) Less than 13% v/v

(C) Less than 14% v/v (D) Less than 15% v/v.

259. *In vitro* studies have reported which of the following activity of *Takrarishta?*

(A) *Antibacterial* (B) Antifungal

(C) Antiviral (D) All of above.

260. *Dasamularishta* and *Amritharishta* have been screened for which of the following activity in experimental animals?

(A) Anti-inflammatory (B) Analgesic

(C) Antipyretic (D) All of above.

261. *Balarishta* has been screened for which of the following activity in experimental animals?

(A) Anti-inflammatory (B) Antioxidant

(C) Antipyretic (D) All of above.

262. Antitussive activity of which of the following formulation has been evaluated in sulphur dioxide induced cough in mice?

(A) *Braham Rasayan* (B) *Kushmandavelha*

(C) *Shirishavaleha* (D) *Vasavaleha.*

263. Which of the following activity has been studied for *Shwasa kuthar Rasa in vitro* model?

(A) Antimicrobial (B) Bronchodilator

(C) Pulmonary antiseptic (D) All of above.

264. The ministry of AYUSH has approved clinical study to access used of which of the following formulations in COVID-19 patients?

(A) *Guduchi Ghana* (B) *Vasa Ghana*

(C) *Vasa Guduchi Ghana* (D) All of above.

265. Ambergris when dissolved in warm alcohol, yields which of the following compound?

(A) Amberein (B) Calcium silicate

(C) Muscone (D) Biliverdin

266. Praval (coral) composition is based on which of the following inorganic lasts?

(A) Calcium carbonate (B) Calcium sulphate

(C) Magnesium carbonate (D) All of the above.

267. Which of the following compound is present in coral?

(A) Iron oxide (B) Silica

(C) Phosphoric acid (D) All of the above.

268. Main inorganic salt present in *Svarjikakshar* is which of the following?

(A) Sodium bicarbonate (B) Sodium carbonate

(C) Sodium chloride (D) Sodium sulphate

269. Which of the following compound is present in *Shilajit*?

(A) Benzocoumarin (B) Benzoic acid

(C) Fulvic acid (D) All of the above.

270. Alum is absorbed in which form among the following?

(A) Albuminate (B) Aluminium sulphate

(C) Potassium sulphate (D) None of the above.

271. *Svarjikakshara* is obtained by the process of incineration of which of the following plants?

(A) *Salsola baryosma* (B) *Salsola kali*

(C) Both of the above (D) None of the above.

272. The chief ingredient of *Yavakshara* is one of the following?

(A) Potassium chloride (B) Potassium carbonate

(C) Potassium bicarbonate (D) Potassium sulphate

273. *Shoraka* (Salt petre) is chemically known as?

(A) Potassium nitrate (B) Potassium chloride

(C) Potassium permanganate (D) All of the above.

274. The main ingredient present in Fuller's earth is known as?

(A) Hydrated aluminium silicate

(B) Aluminium silicate

(C) Aluminium choride

(D) Aluminium sulphate.

275. The chief ingredient of alum is which of the following?

(A) Aluminium sulphate

(B) Potassium sulphate

(C) Compound of aluminium sulphate and potassium sulphate

(D) Calcium carbonate.

276. The chief ingredient of *Hazrul Yahood* (Lime stone) is which of the following?

(A) Calcium silicate (B) Calcium carbonate

(C) Calcium oxide (D) Calcium chloride.

277. The chief chemical component of *Akika* (Agate) is based on which element?

(A) Silica (B) Calcium

(C) Magnesium (D) Manganese.

278. The chief chemical present in *Sangeyashva* (Jade) is based on which element?

(A) Silica (B) Calcium

(C) Magnesium (D) Manganese.

279. Which of the following is used as a cardiac tonic?

(A) *Akika* (Agate) (B) *Kheruva* (Umber)

(C) *Sangeyashva* (Jade) (D) All of the above.

280. The main chemical ingredient of musk oil obtained the process of steam distillation is which one of the following?

(A) Muscone (B) Amberein

(C) Ketone (D) Aldehyde

281. *Badarashma* (Lime stone) is given in the treatment of which of the following diseases?

(A) Kidney stone (B) Pyuria

(C) Dysuria (D) Anuria

282. The therapeutic action of *Badarashma* (Lime stone) is which one of the following?

(A) Diuretic (B) Lithontriptic

(C) Both of the above (D) None of the above.

283. Which of the following compound is found in *Vidalavana*?

(A) Ammonium chloride

(B) Potassium chloride

(C) Ammonium bicarbonate

(D) Potassium bromide.

284. Which of the following are synonyms for *Badarashma* (Lime stone)?

(A) Fossil encrinites (B) Jew's stone

(C) Fossil stone (D) All of the above.

285. *Jahar Mohra* (*Nagapashana*) is compound of which of the following elements?

(A) Silica and magnesium (B) Silica and oxygen

(C) Silica and phosphorus (D) None of the above.

286. *Jahar Mohra* (*Nagapashana*) is beneficial in the treatment of which of the following heart diseases?

(A) Palpitation (B) Cardiac asthenia

(C) Angina pectoris (D) (A) and (B).

287. Which of the following formulation based on *Pravala* is considered to be therapeutically effective?

(A) *Pravala pisthi*

(B) *Pravala bhasam*

(C) *Chandraputita Pravala pisthi*

(D) *Pravala pancha amrita rasa.*

288. Which of the following Ayurvedic books/texts have described the use of *Badarashma* (Lime stone) for the first time?

(A) *Charaka Samhita* (B) *Sushruta Samhita*

(C) *Rasamrita* (D) *Sharangdhar Samhita*

289. The scientific source of *Pravala Mula* is which of the following?

(A) *Tubipora musica* (B) *Helix aspera*

(C) Both of the above. (D) None of the above.

290. The scientific source of *Pravala Shakha* is which of the following?

(A) *Corallium rubrum* (B) *Helix aspera*

(C) Both of the above. (D) None of the above.

291. Which of the following text has described *Godanti* (Gypsum) for the first time?

(A) *Rasatarangini* (B) *Bhavprakash Nighantu*

(C) *Raj Nighantu* (D) *Rasavarana*

292. The chemical formula for *Godanti* (Gypsum) is which of the following?

(A) $CaSO_4.2H_2O$ (B) $CaSO_4$

(C) $CaCO_3$ (D) CaO.

293. *Mrigashringa* contains which of the following compounds?

(A) Free calcium (B) Iron as ferric oxide (FeO_3)

(C) Phosphate and magnesium (D) All of the above.

294. In a clinical trial evaluating potential of *Pravala* formulations on *Amlapitta* (hyperacidity), which showed better result?

(A) *Pravala Shakha Sarjika Kshara Shodhita Bhasma*

(B) *Shakha Shakha Tandulikya Swarasa Shodhita Bhasma*

(C) *Pravala Mula Bhasma Sarjika Kshara Shodhita Bhasma*

(D) *Pravala Mula Bhasma Tandulikya Swarasa Shodhita Bhasma*

295. Clinical efficacy of jatamansin has been evaluated in which of the following diseases?

(A) Hemorrhoids (B) Pilonidal sinus

(C) Fistula in ano (D) Anal fissure

296. Clinical efficacy of nimbidin has been studied in which of the following diseases?

(A) Peptic ulcer (B) Gastric ulcer

(C) Reflux esophagitis (D) Duodenal ulcer

297. A double blind study has reported efficacy of nimbidin in the treatment of which skin disease?

(A) Leucoderma (B) Lichen planus

(C) Psoriasis (D) Scabies

298. What is the exact proportion of elemental calcium in *Muktapisthi*?

(A) 96.4% w/w (B) 95% w/w

(C) 92% w/w (D) 89% w/w

299. What is the exact proportion of elemental calcium and calcium carbonate in *Muktabhasma*?

(A) 40-45% w/w and 99.391% w/w

(B) 45-50% w/w and 99.391% w/w

(C) 50-55% w/w and 99.391% w/w

(D) 55-60% w/w and 99.391% w/w

300. What is the exact proportion of elemental calcium and calcium carbonate in *Pravalbhasma*?

(A) 30.9-43.6 % w/w and 33.40-47.79% w/w

(B) 32.9-43.8 % w/w and 35.40-49.79% w/w

(C) 35.6-44.6 % w/w and 35.40-49.79% w/w

(D) 40.7-45.8 % w/w and 38.45-48.81% w/w

301. Magnesium oxide is present in which of the following formulations?

(A) *Muktabhasma* (B) *Muktapishti*

(C) *Pravalbhasma* (D) *Pravalpishti*

302. Which of the following formulation based on *Nilam* (Sapphire) finds use in Unani System of Medicine?

(A) *Nilampisthi* (B) *Nilambhasam*

(C) Both of the above (D) None of the above.

303. The chemical makeup of *Nilam* (Sapphire) is which of the following?

(A) Al_2O_3 (B) $AlCl_3$

(C) Both of the above (D) None of the above.

304. The chemical makeup of *Gomeda* (Cinnamon stone) is which of the following?

(A) $ZrSiO_4$ (B) $ZnCl_2$

(C) ZnO (D) $ZnSO_4$.

305. The chemical makeup of *Vadurya* (Cat's Eye) is which of the following?

(A) $BeOAlO_3$ (B) $BeCl_2$

(C) Both of the above (D) None of the above.

306. *Nilam* has which of the following properties?

(A) Antimalarial (B) Antiprotozoal

(C) Antifilarial (D) Antibacterial.

307. The upper and lower limit of mercury in *Rasa Sindoora* as per *Rasaratangini* is which of the following?

(A) 82.7-87.1%w/w (B) 84.7-88.1%w/w

(C) 85.7-87.4%w/w (D) 90.7-89.1%w/w.

308. The upper and lower limit of mercury in *Makardwaj* as per *Rasaratangini* is which of the following?

(A) 72.2-76.0%w/w (B) 72.2-76.2%w/w

(C) 72.2-76.4%w/w (D) 72.2-76.6%w/w.

309. The upper and lower limit of mercury in *Rasa Karpura* as per *Rasaratangini* is which of the following?

(A) 64.2-74.6%w/w (B) 66.2-74.8%w/w

(C) 64.2-74.9%w/w (D) 64-2-75.0%w/w.

310. Which of the following inorganic salts are present in *Rasapushpa* as per *Rasaratangini*?

(A) HgO (B) Fe_2O_3

(C) Chloride (D) All of the above.

311. The maximum amount of arsenic present in *Mal Sindoor* as per *Rasaratangini* is which of the following?

(A) 14.30%w/w (B) 14.32%w/w

(C) 14.34%w/w (D) 14.36%w/w

312. The total alkaloidal content involving Physico-Chemical profile of *Puga Khanda* ranged from which of the following values as determined by TLC?

(A) 0.001 to 0.002% w/w (B) 0.002 to 0.003% w/w

(C) 0.002 to 0.004% w/w (D) None of the above.

313. Anticancer activity of *Arkeshwara Rasa* has been demonstrated in which of the following cancers?

(A) Colon (B) Liver

(C) Pancreatic (D) None of the above.

314. Which of the following medicinal plants are included in the red listed medicinal plants?

(A) *Acorus calamus* (B) *Pterocarpus santalinus*

(C) *Rauvolfia serpentina* (D) All of the above.

315. *Triphala* extracts and *Triphala Masi* has shown which of the following activity in a remarkable fashion?

(A) Antiallergic (B) Antidiarrhoeal

(C) Antiprotozoal (D) Hypolipidemic.

316. *Swarna Makshika Bhasam* has shown which of the following activity in experimental studies?

(A) Genotoxic (B) Non-genotoxic

(C) Carconogenic (D) Non-carcinogenic.

317. *Vasant Kusumakar Ras* has shown which of the following activity in experimental studies?

(A) Hypoglycemic (B) Antihyperglycemic

(C) Hyperglycemic (D) Antidiabetic.

318. Which of the following formulations based on *Guduchi* has shown promise in the treatment of obesity?

(A) *Guduchi Kwatha* (B) *Guduchi Satva*

(C) *Guduchyadi churna* (D) *Amritarishta.*

319. A systematic phase 1 study with *Yograj Guggul* reported which type of tolerability in volunteers?

(A) Bad (B) Good

(C) Significant (D) None of above.

320. Which of the formulation based on *guggul* has shown significant antiarthritic and chondroprotective activity?

(A) *Lakshadi guggul* (B) *Simhnada guggul*

(C) *Kaishore guggul* (D) *Mahayograj guggul.*

321. *Gmelina asiatica* root used as substituent for *Gmelina arborea* is an example of which of the following?

(A) Pharmacopoeial drug (B) Extrapharmacopoeial drug

(C) Formulary drug (D) None of above.

322. Decoction of stem bark of *Terminalia arjuna* has been found to be useful in which of the following diseases?

(A) Hypertension (B) Congestive cardiac failure

(C) Refractive heart disease (D) Ischemic heart disease.

323. Which of the following activities have been observed for *Shilajatvadi Lauha* in rat studies?

(A) Anti-diabetic (B) Anti-hyperlipidemic

(C) Both of above (D) None of above.

324. Clinical efficacy of *Vyaghriharitaki Avaleha* has been reported in the management of which disease?

(A) Acute bronchitis (B) Chronic bronchitis

(C) Asthmatic bronchitis (D) All of above.

325. In a comparative study, the hypolipidemic activity of *Arogyavardhini vati* in Triton WR-1339-induced hyperlipidemic rats has been compared with which of the following drug?

(A) Atorvastatin (B) Fenofibrate

(C) Gemofibrozil (D) Simvastatin.

326. *Invitro* studies have reported which of the following activities for *Lodhrasava*?

(A) Alpha-amylase inhibition

(B) Alpha-glucosidase inhibition

(C) Adipogenic suppression (D) All of above.

327. The major ingredient of *Khanjnikari Rasa* is which one of the following?

(A) *Malla Sindoor* (B) *Rasa Karpura*

(C) *Rasa Sindoor* (D) *Suvarna Vanga.*

328. *Kasturi* (musk) is present in which of the following formulations?

(A) *Navratan Rasa* (B) *Vatagajankush Rasa*

(C) *Vatakultantak Rasa* (D) *Vatavidhwansan Rasa.*

329. *Mugdha Rasa* (Grey powder) is indicated in the treatment of which of the following diseases?

(A) Convulsions (B) Diarrhea

(C) Otitis media. (D) Vomiting

330. *Suvarana vanga* is indicated especially in the treatment of which of the following diseases?

(A) Gonorrhea (B) Syphilis

(C) Pyorrhea. (D) All of above.

331. *Hiraka Bhasma* (Diamond calyx) is ingredient of which of the following formulations?

(A) *Mahalaxmivilas Rasa* (B) *Vasankusumakar Rasa*

(C) *Vatalulantak Rasa.* (D) All of above.

332. *Praval Bhasma* (Coral calyx) is ingredient of which of the following formulations?

(A) *Pravalpanchamrita Rasa*

(B) *Vishamjvaratak Lauha*

(C) *Putpakva Vishamjvaratak Lauha*

(D) All of above.

333. Which of the following *bhasma* is present in *Rasraj Rasa*?

(A) *Suvarna* (B) *Rajat*

(C) *Tamra* (D) *Naga.*

334. Which of the following *bhasma* is a hair-coloring agent and treats leucoderma?

(A) *Rajat* (B) *Kasisa*

(C) *Loha* (D) *Praval.*

335. Chemically speaking, *Karpura Shilajit* is which one of the following compounds?

(A) Potassium nitrate (B) Potassium chloride

(C) Potassium sulphate (D) Potassium permanganate.

336. For *rasayana* action, which of the following *Shilajit* is useful?

(A) *Gomutra* (B) *Karpura*

(C) Both of above (D) None of above.

337. National Clinical Management Protocol based on Ayurveda for management of Covid-19 is based on which of the following parameters?

(A) Knowledge from Ayurveda classics and experience from clinical practices

(B) Empirical evidences and biological plausibility

(C) Emerging trends of ongoing clinical studies

(D) All of above.

338. As per National Clinical Management Protocol based on Ayurveda for management of Covid-19 which form of *Ashwagandha* is recommended?

(A) Aqueous extract (B) Alcoholic extract

(C) Hydro-alcoholic extract (D) Fermented product.

339. How many classical medicines have been validated for 70 disease conditions during 2019 by CCRAS?

(A) 80 (B) 100

(C) 120 (D) 140.

340. The Scheme for Integrated Health Research (SIHR) has been drawn up by Department of AYUSH in collaboration with which of the following?

(A) NITI Aayog

(B) Invest India (AGNI Platform)

(C) NITI Aayog and Invest India

(D) None of above.

341. Clinical trial of Ayush-64 and *saptaparna ghana vati* has been carried in which diseases condition?

(A) Falciparum malaria (B) Microfilaremia
(C) Ovale malaria (D) Vivax malaria.

342. Clinical assessment of the effect of Ayush-64 has been studied in which of the following stage of filariais?

(A) Acute (B) Sub acute
(C) Chronic (D) All.

343. Ayush-64 administered orally at which of the following dose level for 30 days did not produce any toxic effects hematological, at the cellular level.

(A) 125 mg/kg (B) 250 mg/kg
(C) 500 mg/kg (D) 750 mg/kg.

344. K.M. Kundnani College of Pharmacy and Pharma Literati launch online course on which of the following subject?

(A) Ethnopharmacology
(B) Phytopharmacovigilance
(C) Patenting and commercialization of herbal products
(D) All of above.

345. As per experts, which of the following discipline should be mandatory in production & marketing of ASU drugs?

(A) Pharmacoepidemiology
(B) Pharmacogenetics
(C) Pharmacovigilance
(D) All of above.

346. Publication tilted 'Research database on Ayurveda, Siddha, other Traditional Medicine and related Sciences' has been pioneered by which of the following?

(A) AYUSH (B) CCRAS
(C) CCIM (D) CCRUM.

347. Pilot evaluation of safety and efficacy of AYUSH 64 for accelerating the recovery has been studied in which of the following diseases?

(A) Dengue fever (B) Chikunguniya

(C) Influenza like illness (D) NIPAH virus.

348. A comparative study compared effect of *Durvadi taila* with which of the following drug in the management of ulcer?

(A) Cetrimide (B) Chlorhexidine

(C) Povidone iodine (D) Tincture benzoin.

349. Clinical studies have been carried out to investigate which effect of *Nimba taila*?

(A) Analgesic and anti-inflammatory

(B) Antiarthritic

(C) Antiscorbutic

(D) Contraceptive.

350. Formulary Specifications of *Ayush Kvatha Curna* has been designed by which of the following department?

(A) Central Council for Research in Ayurvedic Sciences

(B) Central Council for Indian Medicine

(C) Pharmacopoeial Commission for Indian Medicine & Homeopathy

(D) None of above.

351. Pharmacopoeial Monograph of *Ayush Kvatha Curna* has been designed by which of the following department?

(A) Central Council for Research in Ayurvedic Sciences

(B) Central Council for Indian Medicine

(C) Pharmacopoeial Commission for Indian Medicine & Homeopathy

(D) None of above.

352. Field clinical trial of *Nityananda rasa* has been carried out in the treatment of which of the following disease?

(A) Helmenthiasis (B) Filariasis

(C) Malaria (D) Typhoid.

353. Antiulcer activity of *Agnitundirasa* has been compared with of the following drug in shay rat?

(A) Cimetidine (B) Fomentidine

(C) Ranitidine (D) Omeprazole.

354. Role of Putiloha Bhasma has been described in the treatment of which of the following disease?

(A) Diabetes inspidius (B) Diabetes mellitus

(C) Complication of diabetes mellitus

(D) None of above.

355. In an experimental evaluation, which of the following activity has been reported for *Manahshila* (realgar)?

(A) Hypnotic (B) Hypno-sedative

(C) Sedative (D) Tranquillizer.

356. A preliminary study reported pharmacological validation of *Musa paradisiaca bhasma* for which antiulcer activity in albino rats?

(A) Antiulcer (B) Gastro protective

(C) Carminative (D) All of above.

357. The efficacy of *Trikatu Churna* is in treating *Agnimandya* is due to which of the following properties?

(A) Appetite stimulant (B) Digestive

(C) Carminative (D) All of above.

358. The effect of *Trikatu* has been studied on pharmacokinetic profile of which of the following synthetic drugs?

(A) Indometachin (B) Isoniazid

(C) Rifampicin (D) All of above.

359. Drug interaction of which of the following non-steroidal anti-inflammatory drug has been reported with *Trikatu*?

(A) Celecoxib. (B) Diclofenac potassium

(C) Diclofenac sodium (D) Ibuprofen

360. The relative bioavailability of zinc from *Laghumaliniv-asantarasa* has been shown to be how many times as compared to a zinc supplement?

(A) 2 (B) 4

(C) 6 (D) 8.

361. Which of the following method has been developed and validated for estimation of charantin in herbal formulations?

(A) HPLC (B) HPTLC

(C) GC-MS (D) TLC.

362. Which of the following activity of *patol churna* has been demonstrated against experimental gastro-duodenal ulcers in rats?

(A) Cardioprotective (B) Gastroprotective

(C) Hepatoprotective (D) Nephroprotective.

363. Effect of *Dhatriyarishta* in the management of which of the following disease has been investigated?

(A) Iron deficiency anemia (B) Jaundice

(C) Hepatitis (D) All of above.

364. Effect of which of the following formulation has been studied on teratogenic effect of cyfluthrin in experimental model w.s.r. to fetal weight and height?

(A) *Dooshivishari agada* (B) *Shirishadi agada*

(C) *Punranava Mandoor* (D) None of above.

365. A randomized, double blind, placebo controlled pilot trial study investigated effects of *Withania somnifera* in patients of which disease?

(A) Anxiety neurosis (B) Depression

(C) Melancholia (D) Schizophrenia.

366. Randomized placebo-controlled trial of *Mustadi Ghanavati* has been carried in which of the following?

(A) Hyperlipidemia (B) Hypercholesterolemia

(C) Hypertriglyceridemia (D) Dyslipidemia.

367. A preliminary clinical trial of *Vatatvaka curna* has been investigated in the treatment of which of the following disease?

(A) Dysfunctional uterine bleeding.

(B) Leucorrhoea

(C) Menorrhagia (D) Metrorrhagia.

368. A trial reported efficacy of *bhringaraja ghanasatwavati* on the patients of which of the following?

(A) Biliary cirrhosis (B) Hemolytic jaundice

(C) Hepatic cirrhosis (D) Hepatocellular jaundice.

369. In rat study, which of the following activities have been studied for *Laghupanchamula*?

(A) Analgesic and hypnotic (B) Anti-inflammatory

(C) Antidepressant (D) All of above.

370. Clinical trials have been done with sodium nimbidinate with respect to which of the following?

(A) Antianginal (B) Antihypertensive

(C) Diuretic (D) None of above.

371. *In-vitro* study of sodium nimbidinate has been done with respect to which of the following?

(A) Spermopiotic (B) Spermicidal

(C) Both of above (D) None of above.

372. Nimbidin has been investigated for which of the following activities?

(A) Analgesic and antipyretic

(B) Anti-inflammatory and antiarthritic

(C) Gastro protective (D) All of above.

373. Clinical efficacy of *Ashwagandha* has been done in which of the arthritis based on humours?

(A) *Vata* (B) *Pitta*

(C) *Kapha* (D) All of above.

374. Free radical scavenging activity of which dosage form of *Ashwagandha* root has been reported in mice?

(A) Arishta (B) Extract

(C) Oil (D) Powder.

375. Clinical evaluation of *Ashwagandha* has been reported in the management of which of the following disease?

(A) *Ama-vata* (Rheumatoid arthritis)

(B) *Sandhigat vata* (Osteoarthritis)

(C) *Vata-rakta* (Gout) (D) All of above.

376. Randomized clinical trial of which of the following formulation has been carried out in the management of *amavata* (rheumatoid arthritis)?

(A) *Anuvasana vasti* (B) *Kshar vasti*

(C) *Nirhuha vasti* (D) None of the above.

377. A double-blind clinical trial of *Arogyawardhini vati* has been conducted in which of the following disease?

(A) Acute viral hepatitis

(B) Alcoholic hepatitis

(C) Chronic hepatitis

(D) Chronic persistent hepatitis.

378. A randomized placebo controlled study on *Sarasvata choorna* has been conducted in which of the following disease?

(A) General anxiety disorder

(B) Obsessive compulsive disorder

(C) Schizophernia.

(D) Seasonal affective disorder.

379. *Aragvadha satapaka ghrita* is used in the management of which of the following disease?

(A) Leucoderma (B) Lichen planus

(C) Lichen simplex (D) Psoriasis.

380. A clinical study evaluated role of *Kiratatiktadi yoga* in management of which of the following disease?

(A) Leucoderma. (B) Pemphigus

(C) Psoriasis (D) Scabies.

381. Clinical trial of which of the following drug has been done in pemphigus?

(A) *Bacopa monnneria* (B) *Centella asiactica*

(C) *Glycyrrhiza glabra* (D) *Glycyrrhiza uralensis.*

382. The efficacy of *madhu tailik vasti* has been studied in the management of which of the following disease?

(A) Arthritis (B) Carditis

(C) Colitis (D) Hepatitis.

383. Clinical evaluation of *tikta kshira vasti* has been studied in the management of which form of arthritis?

(A) Osteoarthritis (B) Psoriatic arthritis

(C) Rheumatic arthritis (D) Rheumatoid arthritis.

384. A study on the effect of *lekhan-vasti* has been evaluated in cases of which of the following disease?

(A) Essential hypertension

(B) Ischemic heart disease

(C) Congestive cardiac failure

(D) (A) and (B).

385. Therapeutic evaluation of *tuvaraka beeja taila* has been carried out in which skin disease?

(A) Eczema (B) Leucoderma

(C) Psoriasis (D) Scabies.

386. *Agnimukha churna* has been tested for which of the following activity in rats?

(A) Antidiarrhoeal (B) Antiemetic

(C) Gastroprotective (D) Prokinetic.

387. Effect of ethanol extract of *Pathyadya Churna* has been investigated for which of the following activity in rats?

(A) Analgesic (B) Antiarthritic

(C) Anti-inflammatory (D) Uricosuric.

388. Evaluation of which of the following activities of *Avipattikar Churna* has been studied on peptic ulcers in experimental rats?

(A) Anti-Secretory (B) Anti-Ulcerogenic

(C) Both of above (D) None of above.

389. Mast cell stabilizing activity of *Sitopaladi churna* aqueous extract and *Sitopaladi churna* methanolic extract is comparable to which of the following drug?

(A) Sodium cromoglycate (B) Ketotifen

(C) Both of above (D) None of above.

390. Which of the following activity has been reported for *Gokhsuradi Churana* by *in vitro* method?

(A) Antidiuretic (B) Antiurolithiatic

(C) Diuretic (D) Urinary antiseptic.

391. Which of the following medicinal plant has been suggested as pharmacologically effective alternative for *Saraca asoca* in *Asokarishta*?

(A) *Kingiodendron pinnatum* (B) *Polyalthia longifolia*

(C) Both of above (D) None of above.

392. *Chincha Rasa* is used as antidote in which of the following poisoning?

(A) *Ahiphena* (B) *Bhallataka*

(C) *Dhatura* (D) *Langali.*

393. The major withanolide present in the leaves of *Ashwagandha* is which one of the following?

(A) Dihydrowithaferin A (B) Withaferin A

(C) Withanolide Y (D) Withanone.

394. The alkaloid berberine was used earlier in the treatment of which of the following disease?

(A) Condyloma acuminata (B) Gonorrhea

(C) Oriental sore (D) Syphilis.

395. Gazette notification regarding Institute of Training and Research in Ayurveda includes which of the following institute?

(A) Post Graduate Teaching and Research in Ayurveda, Jamnagar

(B) Shree Gulabkunverba Ayurved Mahavidyalaya, Jamnagar

(C) The Indian Institute of Ayurvedic Pharmaceutical Sciences, Jamnagar

(D) All of the above.

396. The Central Government has approved Ayush Day Care therapy centres for Central government employees under which of the following schemes?

(A) CGHS (B) Ayuhsman Bharat

(C) Both (D) None.

397. Scientific Advisory Board for the Pharmacopoiea Commission of Indian Medicine & Homoeopathy is proposed to have a term of how many years?

(A) 1 (B) 2

(C) 3 (D) 4.

398. Scientific Advisory Board for the Pharmacopoiea Commission of Indian Medicine & Homoeopathy shall perform an advisory function to the Central Government, the State Governments and the stakeholders on

(A) The matters of standards,

(B) SOPs (Standard Operating Procedures)

(C) Testing protocols of Ayurveda, Siddha, Unani and Homoeopathy Drugs.

(D) All of the above.

399. Classical drugs in AYUSH include which of the following?

(A) Raw /crude drugs (B) Extracts

(C) Compound formulations

(D) Herbo mineral formulations

(E) All of the above.

400. Under Microbial Load, the limits as prescribed in ASU Pharmacopoeias should be absent for which of the following?

(A) *Staphylococcus aureus* (B) *Salmonella sp.*

(C) *Pseudomonas aeruginosa* (D) *Escherichia coli*

(E) All of the above.

401. The limit prescribed for lead in ASU Pharmacopoeias is which one of the following?

(A) 4 ppm (B) 6 ppm

(C) 8 ppm (D) 10 ppm.

402. The limit prescribed for cadmium in ASU Pharmacopoeias is which one of the following?

(A) 0.01 ppm (B) 0.02 ppm

(C) 0.03 ppm (D) None of the above.

403. The limit prescribed for mercury in ASU Pharmacopoeias is which one of the following?

(A) 1 ppm (B) 2 ppm

(C) 3 ppm (D) None of the above.

404. The limit prescribed for arsenic in ASU Pharmacopoeias is which one of the following?

(A) 1 ppm (B) 2 ppm

(C) 3 ppm (D) None of the above.

405. Which of the following excipient when added to herbal drugs imparts hardness to the tablet?

(A) Alcohol (B) Glycerin

(C) Gum arabic (D) Gum tragacanth.

406. Which of the following excipient imparts smoothness to the resinous substances?

(A) Alcohol (B) Glycerin

(C) Soap powder (D) Wax.

407. For tablets containing volatile oil or phenol, powder of which is of the following herbal drugs is recommended for maintaining consistency of the excipient?

(A) Marshmallow (*Althoea officinalis*)

(B) Country mallow (*Sida cordifolia*)

(C) Licorice (*Glychyrrhiza glabra*)

(D) (A) and (C).

408. Wax is considered to be best excipient for which one of the following although obsolete?

(A) Camphor (B) Creosote

(C) Phenol (D) Volatile oil

(E) All of the above.

409. Which of the following is best excipient for making tablets of *Ahiphena* (*Papaver somniferum*) powder?

(A) Alcohol (B) Glycerin

(C) Water (D) None of above.

410. Ministry of AYUSH and the All Indian Institute of Medical Sciences shall set up which of the following department in AIIMS?

(A) Alternative (B) Complementary

(C) Herbal (D) Integrative.

411. The Union Ministry of Commerce & Industry and the Ministry of Ayush have decided to jointly set up which of the following to boost Ayush exports?

(A) AYSUH Export Promotion Council

(B) Pharmaexil

(C) Herbal Export Promotion Council

(D) All of above.

412. The Centre for Traditional Medicines and Research (CTMR) is engaged in research in which of the following system of medicine?

(A) Ayurveda (B) Homeopathy

(C) Siddha (D) Unani.

413. The Regional Raw Drug Repository (RRDR) for Ayush systems of medicine has been set up by Ministry of AYUSH at which of the following institute?

(A) National Institute of Ayurveda

(B) National Institute of Homeopathy

(C) National Institute of Siddha

(D) National Institute of Unani.

414. In a clinical study, the efficacy of *Kapha Ketu Rasa* has been investigated in which of the following disease?

(A) Acute bronchitis (B) Bronchial asthma

(C) Chronic bronchitis (D) Pneumonia.

415. A study has been conducted to evaluate which of the following activity in favor of *Sanjivani vati*?

(A) Water purification (B) Water-sorption

(C) Oxygen purification (D) All of abovc.

416. A pilot study investigated clinical efficacy of *Sanjivani vati* and *Lashunadi vati* in management of which form of irritable bowel syndrome?

(A) Constipation predominant IBS

(B) Diarrhea predominant IBS

(C) IBS alone

(D) None of above.

417. The publication 'A Focus on Research and Development' targeting fifty years of transforming research and development in Ayurveda has been pioneered by which of the following?

(A) AYUSH (B) CCIM

(C) CCRAS (D) All of above.

418. Which herbal drug was suggested by AYUSH experts as an adjunct to Hydroxychloroquine for possible clinical trial in COVID-19?

(A) *Ashwagandha* (B) *Guduchi*

(C) *Vasa* (D) *Yastimadhu.*

419. A clinical study has evaluated efficacy of *Yavaksharadi vati* and *Panchavalkal kwath* in the management of which of the following disease?

(A) Adenoids (B) Quinsy

(C) Sore throat (D) Tonsillitis.

420. A clinical study has evaluated efficacy of *Virechan* and *Rasnasaptak kwath* in the management of which of the following disease?

(A) Gout (B) Rheumatic arthritis.

(C) Rheumatism (D) Rheumatoid arthritis.

421. Efficacy of *Phaltrikadi kwath* has been evaluated in which of the following disease?

(A) Cardioprotective (B) Hepatoprotective

(C) Nephroprotective (D) All of above.

422. Efficacy of *Panchtikta ghruta* has been evaluated in which of the following disease?

(A) Alcoholic hepatitis (B) Biliary cirrhosis.

(C) Hepatic cirrhosis (D) Viral hepatitis.

423. Efficacy of *Phalatrikadi kwath* and *Arogyavardhini* has been evaluated in which of the following disease?

(A) Alcoholic hepatitis

(B) Biliary cirrhosis.

(C) Hepatic cirrhosis-early stage

(D) Viral hepatitis.

424. A study reported effectiveness of *Triphala kwath* in the management of which of the following disease?

(A) Congestive dysmennorhoea

(B) Dysfunctional uterine bleeding.

(C) Leucorrhoea

(D) Spasmodic dysmennorhoea.

425. Efficacy of *Mansyadi kwath shirodhara* has been reported in which of the following disease?

(A) Anxiety neurosis

(B) Essential hypertension

(C) Mild depression

(D) Severe depression.

426. Which of the following drugs are used as source for Ayurvedic drug *Kakanasa?*

(A) *Martynia annua* L. (Martyniaceae).

(B) *Trichosanthes cucumerina* L. (Cucurbitaceae)

(C) *Asclepias currasavica* L. (Apocynaceae)

(D) *Dicliptera paniculata* (Acanthaceae)

(E) All of above.

427. Which of the following medicinal plant is taken as source of *Nilabhrṇgaraja* in Siddha system of medicine?

(A) *Eclipta alba* L. (Asteraceae)

(B) *Caesulia axillaris* Roxb. (Asteraceae)

(C) *Wedelia chinensis* (Osbeck) Merr. (Asteraceae)

(D) All of above.

428. Which of the following drugs are used as source for Unani drug *Gaozabaan?*

(A) *Anchusa italica* Retz. (Boraginaceae)

(B) *Borago officinalis* Linn. (Boraginaceae)

(C) *Caccinia crassifolia* O. Kuntze. (Boraginaceae)

(D) All of above.

429. Which of the following drugs are used as source for drug *Secacul mishri*?

(A) *Pastinaca secacul* Linn. (Apiaceae)

(B) *Trachydium lehmanni* Benth. (Apiaceae)

(C) *Eryngium caeruleum* Bieb.(Apiaceae)

(D) All of above.

430. Which of the following drugs are used as source for drug *Sugandhbala*?

(A) *Limnophila indica* (Linn.) Druce (Lamiaceae)

(B) *Limnophila rugosa* (Roth.) Merrill (Lamiaceae)

(C) Both of above (D) None of above.

431. Which of the following drugs are used as source for drug *Granthika Tagara*?

(A) Nymphoides macrospermum Vasudevan (*Menyanthaceae*)

(B) *Cryptocoryne spiralis* (Retz.) Fisch. ex Wydl (Araceae)

(C) Both of above

(D) None of above.

432. Which of the following drugs are used as adulterant for *Ativīśā* (*Aconitum heterophyllum* Wall)?

(A) *Chaerophyllum villosum* Wall. ex DC (Apiaceae)

(B) *Cryptocoryne spiralis* (Retz.) Fisch. ex Wydl (Araceae)

(C) Both of above

(D) None of above.

433. Which of the following drugs are used as source for drug *Padamcarini*?

(A) *Nervilia aragoana* (Gaud.) Ridl. (*Ranunculaceae*)

(B) *Habenaria grandifloriformis* Blatter et McCann (Orchidaceae)

(C) *Nervilia plicata* (Andr.) Schltr. (*Ranunculaceae*)

(D) *Nervilia prainiana* (King et Pantl.) Seidenf. Et Smitin (*Ranunculaceae)*

(E) All of above.

434. Which of the following medicinal plants are taken as source for controversial drug *Lakshmana?*

(A) *Ipomoea muricata* (L.) Jacq. (Convolvulaceae)

(B) *Cynoglossum lanceolatum* Forssk. (Boraginaceae)

(C) *Solanum ferox* L. (Convolvulaceae)

(D) All of above.

435. Which of the following medicinal plants are used as adulterants of *Crocus sativus* L.?

(A) *Arnica montana* L. (*Asteraceae*)

(B) *Calendula officinalis* L. (*Asteraceae*)

(C) *Carthamus tinctorius* L. (*Asteraceae*)

(D) *Pulicaria crispa* L. (*Asteraceae*)

(E) All of above.

436. Drug Standardization Programe of CCRAS is being conducted through which of the following peripheral institutes?

(A) CSMRIA&SDD, Chennai

(B) NRIADD, Kolkata

(C) NIAPR, Patiala

(D) NRIASHRD, Gwalior

(E) All of above.

437. Which of the following term is reserved for link between *Prakriti* and modern genomics for development of predictive and personalized medicine?

(A) Ayurgenomics (B) Personalized medicine

(C) Reverse pharmacology (D) Golden Triangle.

438. Clinical studies with *Amalaki-Phyllanthus emblica* Linn. (Euphorbiaceae) has been done in which of the following diseases?

(A) Hypercholsterolemia (B) Dyspepsia

(C) Hyperacidity (D) All of above.

439. INMEDPLAN (Indian medicinal plants database) modules is maintained by which of the following institute?

(A) I-AIM, Institute for Ayurvedic and Integrative medicine

(B) All India Institute of Ayurveda

(C) National Institute of Ayurveda

(D) CCRAS.

440. Encyclopedia on Indian Medicinal Plants is maintained by which of the following institute?

(A) Foundation for Revitalization of Local Health Traditions (FRLHT)

(B) I-AIM, Institute for Ayurvedic and Integrative medicine

(C) All India Institute of Ayurveda

(D) Ministry of AYUSH.

441. *Nighantus* have been classified in how many type?

(A) Lexical *Nighantu* (B) Pharmacological *Nighantu*

(C) Both of above (D) None of above.

442. Which of the following have been as artificial sweeteners in various dosage forms of AYUSH Medicines?

(A) Sucralose (B) Aspartame

(C) Saccharin sodium (D) All of above.

443. A clinical trial of *Ajmodadi churna* and *Yograj Guggul* has been carried in which of the following disease?

(A) Rheumatoid arthritis (B) Rheumatic arthritis

(C) Gout (D) Sciatica.

444. A comparative trial of *Amalaki* and *Yastimadhu churna* has been carried in which of the following disease?

(A) Constipation (B) Duodenal ulcer

(C) Gastric ulcer (B) Gastritis.

445. Government of India made the Good Manufacturing Practice (GMP) mandatory for all AYUSH units in which of the following years?

(A) 2002 (B) 2004

(C) 2006 (D) 2010.

446. Batch Manufacturing Records in AYUSH units must include which of the following?

(A) List of raw materials used,

(B) Quantity obtained from the store,

(C) Tests conducted during the various stages of manufacture

(D) All of above.

447. To verify the finished products in AYUSH units, controlled samples of finished products of each batch should be kept for how many years?

(A) 2 (B) 3

(C) 5 (D) 10.

448. Manufacturers manufacturing patent proprietary AYUSH medicines shall provide specifications and control references in respect of formulatcd drugs fiom which source?

(A) In house (B) Pharmacopoeial

(C) Industrial (D) All of above.

449. Quality control section related to AYUSH manufacturing units should be associated with which of the following in addition to recognized AYUSH degree?

(A) Bachelor of Pharmacy (B) Pharmacgnosy

(C) Chemistry (D) Any one of above.

450. The publication named 'Guidelines for Inspection of GMP Compliance by AYUSH Drug Industry is based on which of the following?

(A) Provisions in the Drugs and Cosmetics Rules, 1945

(B) Ayurvedic Pharmacopoeia of India

(C) Essential Drug List

(D) All of above.

451. Which of the following are exempted from the purview of GMP under IMCC Act, 1970?

(A) Vaidyas, Siddhas and Hakeems

(B) Physicians practicing on basis of experience

(C) AYUSH units established before 2002.

(D) All of above.

452. Minimum manufacturing space required for AYUSH Drug Industry is which one of the following?

(A) 800 Square feet (B) 1000 Square feet

(C) 1200 Square feet (D) 1400 Square feet.

453. Rasaushadhis Related Store as per GMP rules should be what capacity?

(A) 50 Square feet (B) 75 Square feet

(C) 80 Square feet (D) 100 Square feet.

454. In Process Quality Control, which of the following registers should be maintained for ready reference?

(A) Shodhan Register

(B) Bhavana and Putta Register

(C) Grinding Records Register

(D) All of above.

455. The first Current Good Manufacturing Practices (CGMP) facility has been set up in which of the following institute?

(A) CSIR-IIIM, Jammu (B) NIPER, Mohali

(C) CIMAP Lucknow (D) NBRI Lucknow

456. How many Standardized Formulations have been mentioned in Ayurvedic Formulary of India?

(A) 850 (B) 875

(C) 900 (D) 985

457. In case of Asavas and Aristas (fermented products), the upper limit of alcohol as self generated should not exceed?

(A) 10% v/v (B) 12% v/v

(C) 14% v/v (D) 16% v/v.

458. The Department of Health Research has initiated proposal for developing mechanism for recognition of which of the following system/s?

(A) Alternative medicine (B) Complementary medicine

(C) Ethomedicine (D) Phytomedicine.

459. Batch Flower Remedy is included in which system of medicine?

(A) Ayurveda (B) Homeopathy

(C) Siddha (D) Unani.

460. The document titled 'WHO GLOBAL REPORT ON TRADITIONAL AND COMPLEMENTARY MEDICINE' was published in which year?

(A) 2010 (B) 2014

(C) 2017 (D) 2019.

461. Till to date, Minimum Standard Requirement has not been formulated for which of the following by CCIM?

(A) BAMS degree course

(B) MD Ayurveda course

(C) Diploma and degree in Ayurvedic Pharmacy

(D) All of above.

462. Which of the following fellowship is related to Ph.D. courses in A/U/S/H?

(A) Ph.D. Fellowship/Senior Research Fellowship

(B) Ph.D. Fellowship/Junior Research Fellowship (Non-AYUSH)

(C) FITM-AYUSH Fellowship

(D) All of above.

463. Which of the following disciplines have been included in Ph.D. Fellowship/Junior Research Fellowship (Non-AYUSH)?

(A) Biological sciences (B) Chemical sciences

(C) Physical sciences (D) All of above.

464. Which of the following postgraduate qualifications related to Ayurvedic Pharmacy is not part of UGC specified degrees?

(A) M. Pharm-Dravyaguna

(B) M. Pharm-Rasa Shastra

(C) Ph.D. Ayurvedic Pharmacy

(D) All of above.

465. D. Pharm (Upvaid) courses in Punjab State are recognized by which of the following?

(A) Board of Ayurveda and Unani Systems of Punjab

(B) Central Council of Indian Medicine

(C) Punjab State Faculty of Ayurvedic and Unani Systems of Medicine

(D) State Department of AYUSH.

466. As per latest CCIM gazette notification, shalya (surgery) and shalakya (ENT) professionals have been permitted to conduct surgery in how many diseases?

(A) 40 (B) 44

(C) 48 (D) 52.

467. Education and practice related to which of the following is not under the purview of Central Council of Indian Medicine?

(A) Ayurveda (B) Homeopathy

(C) Siddha (D) Yoga and Naturopathy.

468. Application of nanotechnology in AYUSH research is at which regulatory level?

(A) Approved (B) Clinical

(C) Non-clinical (D) Toxicological.

469. Which of the following officer is responsible for forwarding new application for grant of license of manufacturing?

(A) Ayurvedic Medical Officer

(B) District Ayurvedic Officer

(C) Director AYUSH

(D) Deputy Director AYUSH.

470. The book titled 'Legal Status of ASU Medicines' has been pioneered by which of the following?

(A) Central Council of Indian Medicine

(B) Central Council for Research in Ayurvedic Sciences

(C) Department of AYUSH

(D) Pharmacopoeial Laboratory of Indian Medicine.

471. Which of the following abbreviations is obsolete/historical importance w.r.t to AYUSH system of medicine?

(A) ASU (B) ISM

(C) ISM&H (D) All of above.

472. The new abbreviation to Ministry of AYUSH after recognition of Amchi System of Medicine is which of the following?

(A) AYUSH&A (B) AASU

(C) ISM&H (D) None of above.

473. Out of the following, which system of medicine is popular in South India?

(A) Amchi (B) Homeopathy

(C) Siddha (D) Unani.

474. The equivalent nomenclature prescribed by Central Council of Indian Medicine about M.D. (Ay.)-*Dravyaguna* is which one of the following?

(A) Herbal Materia Medica & pharmacology

(B) Materia Medica & pharmacology

(C) Materia Medica & pharmacognosy

(D) Materia Medica & phytopharmacognosy.

475. A person with M.D. (Ay.)-*Dravyaguna* qualification is eligible to teach which of the following subjects?

(A) *Agadtantra* (B) *Kayachikitsa*

(C) *Rasa Shastra* (D) (A) and (B).

476. Which of the following postgraduate qualification(s) are eligible to work as a technical person in Ayurvedic pharmacy?

(A) M.D. (Ay.)-*Agad Tantra*

(B) M.D. (Ay.)-*Dravyaguna*

(C) M.D. (Ay.)-*Rasa Shastra*

(D) (B) and (C).

477. Out of the following chemistry subjects, which is more relevant to study of *Dravyaguna*?

(A) Inorganic chemistry (B) Medicinal chemistry

(C) Organic chemistry (C) Phytochemistry.

478. Which of the following medicinal plant is major ingredient of herbo-mineral formulation *Arogyavardhini Rasa*?

(A) *Ativisha* (B) *Bhallatak*

(C) *Kutki* (D) *Pippali.*

479. Direct Central Registration is done by Central Council of Indian Medicine in which of the following case?

(A) When state registration has been cancelled

(B) When no state registration board exists

(C) When enrolment certificate becomes obsolete

(D) All of above.

480. Decoction of which of the following herb prepared on gentle fire is prescribed as a remedy for sciatica?

(A) *Aprajita*-blue variety (B) *Aprajita*-White variety

(C) *Parijata* (D) *Salai-guggul.*

481. Bromhexine is derivative of which of the following secondary metabolites?

(A) Adathodine (B) Adathodic acid

(C) Vasicine (D) Vasicinol.

482. Withaferin-A accumulate in which part of *Ashwagandha*?

(A) Flower (B) Leaves

(C) Roots (D) Shoots.

483. Which of the following alcoholic preparation has been mentioned in *Caraka Samhita* only?

(A) *Dhatkyadiarishta* (B) *Madhvasva*

(C) *Madhvarishta* (D) *Takrarishta.*

484. Which of the following anticancer compound has been found in *Talishpatra*?

(A) 3-baccatin (B) Essential oil

(C) Taxine (D) Taxol.

485. Asparagin present in genus Asparagus has which of the following medicinal activity?

(A) Cardiotonic (B) Diuretic

(C) Laxative (D) Lithontriptic.

486. Which of the following compound (s) has/have antibiotic property?

(A) Berberine (B) Guggulsterone

(C) Ptergyospermin (D) (A) and (B).

487. Which of the following body conducts entrance examination, National Eligibility Entrance Test (NEET) for admission to AYUSH undergraduate courses?

(A) AYUSH (B) CCIM

(C) CCRAS (D) NTA.

488. All India Post Graduate Entrance Test (AIAPGET) leading to admission in AYUSH postgraduate courses is conducted by which of the following?

(A) ASUTAB (B) ASUDCC

(C) AIIA, New Delhi (D) NIA, Jaipur.

489. Which of the following alkaloid present in the root of *Sarpagandha* has antiarrthymic activity?

(A) Ajmaline (B) Ajmalicine

(C) Reserpine (D) Serpentine.

490. Which of the following medicinal plant is used as antidote to *Urtica diocia* poisoning?

(A) *Artemisia absinthum* (B) *Artemisia annua*

(C) *Artemisia martima* (D) *Artemisia vulgaris.*

491. Ministry of AYUSH consults which of the following for draft notification for inclusion of degree in 2nd schedule?

(A) CCIM (B) CCRAS

(C) MoHFW (D) All of above.

492. Which of the following subjects are not full-fledged subjects as per syllabus prescribed by CCIM?

(A) Ayurvedic dietetics (B) Naturopathy

(C) Pharmacology (D) All of above.

493. Pharmacology is included as topic of study in which of the following subjects in Ayurveda UG/PG curriculum?

(A) *Agad Tantra* (B) *Dravyaguna*

(C) *Rasa Shastra* (D) *Prasuti Tantra.*

494. Which of the following subjects have been carved out of Ashtangayurved as full-fledged subjects?

(A) *Dravyaguna* (B) *Rasa Shastra*

(C) *Sharira Rachana* (D) All of above.

495. *Nityanand Rasa* is the formulation of choice in the treatment of which of the following disease?

(A) Malaria (B) Filariasis

(C) Typhoid (D) Typhus.

496. Which of the following formulations are used in the treatment of respiratory tract diseases?

(A) *Sitopladi churna* (B) *Shrngyadi churna*

(C) *Talishadi churna* (D) *All of above.*

497. Use of *Avipatikar churna* is contraindicated in which of the following disease?

(A) Diabetes (B) Hypertension

(C) Renal calculi (D) All of above.

498. Which of the following formulations are widely used in the treatment of thyroid diseases?

(A) *Kanchnar guggul* (B) *Shankhpushpyadi churna*

(C) *Lakshadi churna* (D) (A) and (B).

499. Which of the following is claimed to be non-narcotic among opium alkaloids?

(A) Morphine (B) Narciene

(C) Noscapine (D) Paparverine.

500. Which of the following formulations are based on opium?

(A) *Ahiphenasva* (B) Tincture opii camphorata

(C) Tincture laudanum (D) All of above.

501. Among the following formulations which is useful in the treatment of skin diseases?

(A) *Abhyarishta* (B) *Lohasva*

(C) *Kanakarishta* (D) *Sarivasva.*

502. *Kumaryasva* suits best with which of the following formulation in the treatment of amenorrhea?

(A) *Navyas lauha* (B) *Punranava Mandura*

(C) *Rajpravatini vati* (D) *Tapyadi lauha.*

503. Use of *Asocarishta* is contraindicated with which of the following formulation?

(A) *Kumaryasva* (B) Rajpravatini vati

(C) Both (D) None.

504. *Pushyanag churna* is used in the treatment of which of the following disease?

(A) Leucorrhoea (B) Menorrhagia

(C) Metrorrhagia (D) All of above.

505. *Rohitukarishta* has been successfully used in the treatment of which form of cancer?

(A) Liver cancer (B) Esophageal cancer

(C) Intestine cancer (D) Stomach cancer.

506. Andrographaloide content in *Andrographis paniculata* is determined by which of the following method?

(A) HPLC (B) HPTLC

(C) Gravimetery (D) TLC.

507. Alkaloid present in kurchi bark responsible for antiprotozoal action is which one of the following?

(A) Aconitine (B) Atisine

(C) Atropine (D) Connesine.

508. Which of the following formulations are used in the treatment of amoebic dysentery?

(A) *Dadimbashtak churna* (B) *Kutajarishta*

(C) *Kutajghan vati* (D) All of above.

509. Which of the following alcoholic preparation is used in the treatment of heart ailments?

(A) *Arjunarishta* (B) *Dhatkyadiarishta*

(C) *Lohasva* (D) *Kumaryasva.*

510. Which of the following formulations are used in the treatment of kidney ailments?

(A) *Gokshuradi guggul* (B) *Gokshuradi kwath*

(C) *Punarnavadi kwath* (D) All of above.

511. Which of the following diseases have connection with *Kumarbhritya*?

(A) *Kshiralsak* (B) *Kukunak*

(C) *Parigarbhik* (D) All of above.

512. Which of the following alcoholic formulation is used in *Kumarbhritya* practice?

(A) *Arvindasva* (B) *Baboolarishta*

(C) *Madhukasva* (D) *Sarivasava.*

513. Which of the following disease is incurable as per Ayurvedic fundamental principles?

(A) *Alsak* (B) *Dandalasak*

(C) *Visuchika* (D) *Vilambika.*

514. Which of the following type of *grahani* is difficult to cure?

(A) *Vataja*
(B) *Pittaja*
(C) *Kaphaja*
(D) *Sangrahani.*

515. The disease in which gurgling sound is heard from the intestine is known as?

(A) *Vataja*
(B) *Pittaja*
(C) *Kaphaja*
(D) *Ghatiyantra grahani.*

ANSWERSHEET

1 **(A)**	2 **(A)**	3 **(A)**	4 **(C)**	5 **(B)**	6 **(B)**	7 **(A)**	8 **(D)**	9 **(D)**	10 **(A)**
11 **(C)**	12 **(A)**	13 **(A)**	14 **(A)**	15 **(A)**	16 **(B)**	17 **(A)**	18 **(A)**	19 **(A)**	20 **(B)**
21 **(A)**	22 **(A)**	23 **(A)**	24 **(D)**	25 **(D)**	26 **(B)**	27 **(D)**	28 **(B)**	29 **(B)**	30 **(A)**
31 **(A)**	32 **(B)**	33 **(B)**	34 **(B)**	35 **(A)**	36 **(A)**	37 **(A)**	38 **(A)**	39 **(A)**	40 **(E)**
41 **(B)**	42 **(C)**	43 **(B)**	44 **(D)**	45 **(D)**	46 **(D)**	47 **(D)**	48 **(B)**	49 **(A)**	50 **(A)**
51 **(B)**	52 **(A)**	53 **(A)**	54 **(A)**	55 **(B)**	56 **(C)**	57 **(A)**	58 **(A)**	59 **(A)**	60 **(B)**
61 **(B)**	62 **(A)**	63 **(A)**	64 **(A)**	65 **(A)**	66 **(A)**	67 **(A)**	68 **(B)**	69 **(A)**	70 **(B)**
71 **(D)**	72 **(D)**	73 **(C)**	74 **(D)**	75 **(D)**	76 **(B)**	77 **(B)**	78 **(A)**	79 **(D)**	80 **(D)**
81 **(D)**	82 **(D)**	83 **(A)**	84 **(A)**	85 **(A)**	86 **(C)**	87 **(D)**	88 **(A)**	89 **(C)**	90 **(B)**
91 **(D)**	92 **(D)**	93 **(D)**	94 **(C)**	95 **(C)**	96 **(C)**	97 **(C)**	98 **(D)**	99 **(D)**	100 **(B)**
101 **(D)**	102 **(B)**	103 **(D)**	104 **(A)**	105 **(A)**	106 **(A)**	107 **(A)**	108 **(A)**	109 **(A)**	110 **(A)**
111 **(A)**	112 **(C)**	113 **(D)**	114 **(A)**	115 **(A)**	116 **(B)**	117 **(A)**	118 **(A)**	119 **(A)**	120 **(B)**
121 **(A)**	122 **(A)**	123 **(C)**	124 **(A)**	125 **(B)**	126 **(A)**	127 **(B)**	128 **(B)**	129 **(C)**	130 **(A)**
131 **(D)**	132 **(A)**	133 **(B)**	134 **(D)**	135 **(D)**	136 **(D)**	137 **(D)**	138 **(B)**	139 **(A)**	140 **(A)**
141 **(B)**	142 **(E)**	143 **(D)**	144 **(C)**	145 **(B)**	146 **(D)**	147 **(A)**	148 **(D)**	149 **(A)**	150 **(D)**
151 **(A)**	152 **(C)**	153 **(B)**	154 **(A)**	155 **(D)**	156 **(E)**	157 **(C)**	158 **(D)**	159 **(D)**	160 **(E)**
161 **(D)**	162 **(D)**	163 **(A)**	164 **(D)**	165 **(B)**	166 **(A)**	167 **(A)**	168 **(A)**	169 **(D)**	170 **(A)**
171 **(A)**	172 **(A)**	173 **(A)**	174 **(A)**	175 **(C)**	176 **(A)**	177 **(A)**	178 **(D)**	179 **(A)**	180 **(C)**
181 **(D)**	182 **(B)**	183 **(D)**	184 **(B)**	185 **(B)**	186 **(D)**	187 **(A)**	188 **(A)**	189 **(A)**	190 **(A)**
191 **(B)**	192 **(A)**	193 **(B)**	194 **(B)**	195 **(A)**	196 **(A)**	197 **(D)**	198 **(A)**	199 **(A)**	200 **(A)**
201 **(B)**	202 **(A)**	203 **(B)**	204 **(A)**	205 **(C)**	206 **(A)**	207 **(C)**	208 **(B)**	209 **(B)**	210 **(A)**
211 **(D)**	212 **(D)**	213 **(B)**	214 **(C)**	215 **(C)**	216 **(C)**	217 **(A)**	218 **(C)**	219 **(B)**	220 **(B)**
221 **(C)**	222 **(C)**	223 **(A)**	224 **(A)**	225 **(A)**	226 **(A)**	227 **(C)**	228 **(B)**	229 **(A)**	230 **(A)**
231 **(D)**	232 **(C)**	233 **(C)**	234 **(A)**	235 **(A)**	236 **(A)**	237 **(A)**	238 **(D)**	239 **(D)**	240 **(C)**
241 **(C)**	242 **(C)**	243 **(B)**	244 **(D)**	245 **(A)**	246 **(C)**	247 **(B)**	248 **(A)**	249 **(A)**	250 **(A)**
251 **(D)**	252 **(A)**	253 **(D)**	254 **(D)**	255 **(A)**	256 **(A)**	257 **(A)**	258 **(A)**	259 **(C)**	260 **(B)**
261 **(C)**	262 **(A)**	263 **(D)**	264 **(A)**	265 **(D)**	266 **(A)**	267 **(D)**	268 **(A)**	269 **(C)**	270 **(A)**

271 **(A)** 272 **(A)** 273 **(C)** 274 **(A)** 275 **(A)** 276 **(A)** 277 **(A)** 278 **(A)** 279 **(A)** 280 **(C)**

281 **(A)** 282 **(D)** 283 **(A)** 284 **(D)** 285 **(C)** 286 **(C)** 287 **(C)** 288 **(C)** 289 **(A)** 290 **(A)**

291 **(A)** 292 **(A)** 293 **(D)** 294 **(A)** 295 **(A)** 296 **(D)** 297 **(C)** 298 **(A)** 299 **(A)** 300 **(A)**

301 **(C)** 302 **(A)** 303 **(A)** 304 **(A)** 305 **(A)** 306 **(A)** 307 **(A)** 308 **(A)** 309 **(A)** 310 **(A)**

311 **(A)** 312 **(C)** 313 **(C)** 314 **(D)** 315 **(B)** 316 **(B)** 317 **(B)** 318 **(A)** 319 **(B)** 320 **(A)**

321 **(B)** 322 **(B)** 323 **(B)** 324 **(B)** 325 **(B)** 326 **(D)** 327 **(A)** 328 **(C)** 329 **(B)** 330 **(A)**

331 **(A)** 332 **(D)** 333 **(A)** 334 **(B)** 335 **(A)** 336 **(A)** 337 **(D)** 338 **(A)** 339 **(D)** 340 **(C)**

341 **(B)** 342 **(A)** 343 **(C)** 344 **(C)** 345 **(C)** 346 **(B)** 347 **(C)** 348 **(C)** 349 **(D)** 350 **(C)**

351 **(C)** 352 **(B)** 353 **(C)** 354 **(C)** 355 **(B)** 356 **(A)** 357 **(A)** 358 **(D)** 359 **(C)** 360 **(D)**

361 **(B)** 362 **(B)** 363 **(A)** 364 **(A)** 365 **(D)** 366 **(A)** 367 **(B)** 368 **(D)** 369 **(A)** 370 **(C)**

371 **(B)** 372 **(D)** 373 **(A)** 374 **(D)** 375 **(A)** 376 **(B)** 377 **(A)** 378 **(A)** 379 **(D)** 380 **(C)**

381 **(C)** 382 **(C)** 383 **(A)** 384 **(D)** 385 **(A)** 386 **(C)** 387 **(A)** 388 **(C)** 389 **(C)** 390 **(B)**

391 **(A)** 392 **(D)** 393 **(B)** 394 **(C)** 395 **(D)** 396 **(A)** 397 **(C)** 398 **(D)** 399 **(E)** 400 **(E)**

401 **(D)** 402 **(C)** 403 **(A)** 404 **(A)** 405 **(C)** 406 **(A)** 407 **(D)** 408 **(E)** 409 **(D)** 410 **(D)**

411 **(A)** 412 **(C)** 413 **(C)** 414 **(B)** 415 **(B)** 416 **(B)** 417 **(C)** 418 **(A)** 419 **(D)** 420 **(D)**

421 **(B)** 422 **(D)** 423 **(C)** 424 **(C)** 425 **(B)** 426 **(E)** 427 **(B)** 428 **(D)** 429 **(D)** 430 **(C)**

431 **(C)** 432 **(C)** 433 **(E)** 434 **(D)** 435 **(E)** 436 **(E)** 437 **(A)** 438 **(D)** 439 **(A)** 440 **(A)**

441 **(C)** 442 **(D)** 443 **(A)** 444 **(B)** 445 **(A)** 446 **(D)** 447 **(C)** 448 **(D)** 449 **(D)** 450 **(A)**

451 **(A)** 452 **(C)** 453 **(D)** 454 **(D)** 455 **(A)** 456 **(D)** 457 **(A)** 458 **(D)** 459 **(D)** 460 **(C)**

461 **(D)** 462 **(D)** 463 **(C)** 464 **(B)** 465 **(D)** 466 **(D)** 467 **(B)** 468 **(C)** 469 **(B)** 470 **(D)**

471 **(D)** 472 **(C)** 473 **(C)** 474 **(B)** 475 **(C)** 476 **(C)** 477 **(B)** 478 **(B)** 479 **(D)** 480 **(B)**

481 **(D)** 482 **(D)** 483 **(C)** 484 **(B)** 485 **(A)** 486 **(A)** 487 **(D)** 488 **(B)** 489 **(D)** 490 **(B)**

491 **(D)** 492 **(D)** 493 **(D)** 494 **(C)** 495 **(D)** 496 **(D)** 497 **(C)** 498 **(B)** 499 **(A)** 500 **(A)**

501 **(C)** 502 **(D)** 503 **(D)** 504 **(A)** 505 **(D)** 506 **(D)** 507 **(A)** 508 **(B)** 509 **(D)** 510 **(D)**